PRAYER REFLECTIONS FOR GROUP MEETINGS

Donal Harrington

Prayer Reflections
for Group Meetings

A PARISH AND MINISTRY RESOURCE

the columba press

First published in 2004 by

the columba press

55A Spruce Avenue, Stillorgan Industrial Park, Blackrock, Co Dublin

Cover by Bill Bolger
Origination by The Columba Press
Printed in Ireland by Colour Books Ltd, Dublin

ISBN 1 85607 441 2

Acknowledgements

Scripture quotations are from the New Revised Standard Version Bible, copyright © 1989, by the Division of Christian Education of the National Council of the Churches of Christ in the United States of America. All rights reserved. Used by permission.

Thanks are due to the following for permission to use their copyright material: Doubleday, a division of Random House, for a quotation from *Conjectures of a Guilty Bystander* by Thomas Merton, © 1966 by The Abbey of Gethsemani; the editor of *The Furrow* for a quotation from Thomas Waldron; Richard Holloway for a quotation from his *Doubts and Loves*, published by Canongate, Edinburgh in 2001; the estate of R. S. Thomas for a quotation from 'The Kingdom' from his *Collected Poems 1945-1990*.

The author also gratefully acknowledges the kind permission of Donagh O'Shea OP and Anne Daly to use their work.

We have made every effort to trace copyright and to seek permission to use quotations. If any involuntary infringement of copyright has occurred, we offer our apologies and will correct the omission in future editions.

Contents

Preface   8

Spirit   10
Our Parish Dream   12
There is Enough   14
Parables for a Searching Church   16
Thanks for our Ministry   18
Love is our Creed   20
Living the Eucharist   22
At the Centre of our Being   24
A Prayer for Wisdom   26
Our Baptism   28
Building Our Parish   30
Adult Faith   32
Breath Came into Them   34
Paths   36
Bringing People to Jesus (Saint Andrew, 30 November)   38
Gifts that Differ   40
Hospitality   42
Advent Prayer   44
Annunciation (25 March)   46
Be Opened!   48
Our Call to Care   50
The Body of Christ   52
Be Seen and Unseen   54

Being Ministered to	56
The Fruits of the Spirit	58
Meditation – for an Evening Meeting	60
A Listening Heart	62
Collaboration then and now	64
For Widowed and Separated People	66
Reaching Out and Reaching In	68
Evangelisation	70
Setting Out	72
The Kingdom	74
A Prayer for Parish Visitation	76
Pastoral Planning	78
Resurrection	80
Be Still and Know	82
What is a Parish for?	84
Service	86
Morning	88
You are …	90
Witness	92
Does God Listen?	94
Meditation: Embodied Me	96
All Ministries are Equal	98
Our Vocation to Love	100
Prayer for the Year Ahead	102
Spring Rain	104
Remembering our Confirmation	106
Our Names	108
Welcome	110
The Trinity Within	112
Our Parish	114
Matthew, Evangelist (21 September)	116

Mark, Evangelist (25 April)   118
Luke, Evangelist (18 October)   120
John, Evangelist (27 December)   122
Our Commitments   124
Reconciliation – Church   126
Christians are Missionaries   128
For Older People   130
The Spirit of Partnership   132
Offertory   134
Saints and Souls (November)   136
Justice   138
Planning in the Parish   140
How does Easter Begin? (1)   142
How does Easter Begin? (2)   144
Preparing for a Parish Assembly   146
Visiting in the Parish   148
Care and Compassion   150
God Words   152
Letting Go   154
Paradoxes   156
Baptism Community   158

References   160
Index of Themes and Names   162
Index of Scripture References   164

Preface

I have called this a book of 'prayer reflections'. By this title I want to suggest that the texts in the book can serve a variety of purposes within a group meeting.

Sometimes the purpose is *prayer together*. There might be a moment of quiet to begin with, or after reading a text from scripture or elsewhere. There might be shared prayer or intercessions. Through such prayer, the group is focusing on the Spirit of Jesus who is the heart of its work.

Sometimes the purpose is *personal sharing*. The text itself is presented as a stimulus for members of the group to share from their own experience. It might be their experience of Christian living, or their experience of ministry, or their experience of participating in the group itself and its work.

Sometimes the purpose is *reflective discussion*. Here the text is an invitation for people to enter into conversation about its theme. That conversation, in turn, may put the spotlight on some particular aspect of the ministry the group is engaged in, so as to deepen their appreciation of it.

I hope that using the texts in such varied ways will enrich the meetings of the group and deepen the experience of ministry, whether in the parish or elsewhere.

Such prayer-reflection is intimately linked to mission. The Christian community today has to put itself forward. It cannot be content to just 'tick over'. It has to deliberately act for the bringing about of God's kingdom. It has to organise itself for mission.

This puts demands on the group itself. The group has to become aware of itself. It has to know who it is and why it exists. It has to put words on this, its identity and role. Prayer-reflection feeds into this, helping the group resource itself for mission and ministry.

Another way of putting this is to say that, in prayer-reflection, the group is taking care of itself. Most of the group's time is taken up with tasks, with business, with things to do. But, as the saying goes, 'you cannot feed the world from an empty dish'. By taking time to resource itself, the group becomes God's resource in the world.

I would like to refer readers to the introduction to the previous volume, *Prayer for Parish Groups* (Donal Harrington and Julie Kavanagh, Columba, 1998). The preface to that book includes a step-by-step guide to preparing and leading the group prayer. This is what makes the *text* of the prayer into an *experience* of prayer for the group.

I would like to thank the people in the parish groups with whom I have shared many of these prayer reflections. They continue to inspire me about the power of the renewal we are engaged in. And I would like to thank Sinead, my wife, for accompanying me in putting this book together.

I wish to dedicate the book to Eoin Cooke, my very dear friend, who died in November 2001.

Spirit

Let our hearts and minds be filled with God's holy Spirit
which has guided creation since the beginning,
which remained with Jesus in his desert and in his dying,
which has been poured out on the world through his rising,
which animates the whole Christian community,
which inspires our discipleship,
which shapes the providence in our lives,
all the dying and rising of our spirit.

Scripture
The Spirit searches everything,
even the depths of God.
For what human being knows what is truly human
except the human spirit that is within?
So also no one comprehends what it truly God's
except the Spirit of God.
Now we have received not the spirit of the world,
but the Spirit that is from God,
so that we may understand
the gifts bestowed on us by God.
(1 Corinthians 2:10-12)

The Spirit helps us in our weakness;
for we do not know how to pray as we ought,
but that very Spirit intercedes
with sighs too deep for words.
And God, who searches the heart,
knows what is the mind of the Spirit
because the Spirit intercedes for the saints
according to the will of God.
(Romans 8:26-27)

The wind blows where it chooses
and you hear the sound of it
but you do not know
where it comes from
or where it goes.
So it is with everyone
who is born of the Spirit.
(John 3:8)

Reflection
In Christ Jesus, my spirit and God's Spirit
are mysteriously one.
As I reflect on Spirit
I centre in on my innermost self.

Prayer
Lord, inspire us with your Spirit;
keep us faithful and keep us hopeful.

Lord, inspire us with your Spirit
and enlighten the eyes of our minds.

Lord, inspire us with your Spirit
and bring to life the dream in our hearts.

Glory be ...

Our Parish Dream

Scripture
Jesus said:
'I came that they may have life
and have it abundantly.'
(John 10:10)

'I came to bring fire to the earth
and how I wish it were already kindled!'
(Luke 12:49)

Reflection
What is a parish? A place yes,
but not just a geographical place.
A 'place' where people find God
and where community happens,
centred on Jesus.

Parish is where Jesus' life continues,
where his dream lives on,
where his fire still burns,
where his passion still throbs
in our hearts.

Prayers
We pray that God's Spirit may bring us
to share ever more deeply
in the sense of mission and purpose
that filled the heart of Jesus.

Response: Lord, ignite your fire within us

May the truth of the gospel teaching
that each of us is loved unreservedly by God
sink into the hearts of all our parishioners
and bring joy and peace into their lives.

May all in our parish know that they belong
and experience the support
of true Christian community;
may all, whatever their situation, feel included
and appreciated for who they are.

May the Eucharist we celebrate together
be the source and the summit of our Christian lives,
nourishing us on our spiritual path,
healing us in our struggles,
challenging us in our daily living
and a real celebration of Christ living among us.

Spirit of God, inflame our hearts;
may our faith be expressed in action,
may our energy be poured
into making your dream come true,
your dream of a people alive with the joy of your love.

Glory be …

There is Enough

Reflection
You must bring him everything!
Your dreams, your successes, your rejoicing.
And if you have little to rejoice over,
bring him that little.
And if your life seems only like
a heap of fragments,
bring him the fragments.
And if you have only empty hands,
bring him your empty hands.
Shattered hopes are his material;
in his hands all is made good.
(Source unknown)

Scripture
When it was evening the disciples came to him and said,
'This is a deserted place and the hour is now late;
send the crowds away so that they may go into the villages
and buy food for themselves.'
Jesus said, 'They need not go away;
you give them something to eat.'
They said, 'We have nothing here but five loaves and two fish.'
And he said, 'Bring them here to me.'
Then he ordered the crowds to sit down on the grass.
Taking the five loaves and the two fish,
he looked up to heaven and blessed and broke the loaves
and gave them to the disciples
and the disciples gave them to the crowds.
And all ate and were filled.
(Matthew 14:15-20)

Prayer
The disciples said, 'But all we have is …'
and then discovered that there was enough.

We find ourselves feeling the same,
such great challenges facing our church and parish,
so few who seem to be interested,
we begin to say, 'But all we have is …'
We start to feel helpless, inadequate;
we begin to think that there isn't enough.

But Jesus, who said to the disciples,
'You give them something to eat'
speaks to us too, saying, 'You have something to give –
your faith, your commitment, your energy –
and the little you have is enough.'

Jesus, teach us the miracle of your presence,
that with your power amongst us, there is enough.
Teach us that the little we have is enough,
enough to be transformed by your power
into a source of new life for your people.

Glory be …

Parables for a Searching Church

These are some of the unnamed figures
who people the events and stories of the gospel.
We imagine how they felt and reflect on
what they might have to say to our searching church.

The sower
You know me, though you do not know my name.
I am the sower. What I have – all I have – is a seed.
I'm not always sure what kind of ground is before me,
whether it be rocky or thorny or fertile.
Sometimes I'm discouraged by so much inhospitable earth.
I've to keep reminding myself of the potential of the seed.

The woman at the well
You know me, though you do not know my name.
I am the woman who went to the well.
I am dizzy with confusion.
I see people coming to believe and it seems to be because of me.
All I did was tell them my story, about my encounter.
It's hard to understand how my story could be changing others.

The labourer
You know me, though you do not know my name.
I am the labourer sent out to the harvest.
I do not know what welcome awaits me, if any.
I feel like a lamb among wolves.
I am told to carry no purse or haversack or sandals.
All I bring is myself and the power of the one who sends me.

The blind man
You know me, though you do not know my name.
I am the blind man. I am being led away from the noise.
I feel the wet hands rubbing my eyes.
I look up and am beginning to see – but only beginning.
Things are blurred for me.
I wait for the hands to touch my eyes again.

The widow
You know me, though you do not know my name.
I am the widow. I have almost nothing to give.
Others around me seem to be oozing resources and riches.
I will give what I have, but I feel so inadequate.
I am told to realise that what I give is everything.

Quiet / Sharing
What echoes in you?
What can you identify with?

Prayer
We believe in you, God our creator;
we know that your creativity flows out from us.

We love you, Jesus, our intimate companion;
we feel your compassion welling within us.

We hope in you, life-giving Spirit;
we quicken with anticipation of all that you promise.

From the depths of our hearts you bind us together;
may we bring forth fruit for the life of the world.

Thanks for our Ministry

Scripture
On the way to Jerusalem Jesus was going through
the region between Samaria and Galilee.
As he entered a village, ten lepers approached him.
Keeping their distance they called out, saying,
'Jesus, Master, have mercy on us.'
When he saw them he said to them,
'Go and show yourselves to the priests.'
And as they went they were made clean.
Then one of them, when he saw that he was healed,
turned back, praising God with a loud voice.
He prostrated himself at Jesus' feet and thanked him.
And he was a Samaritan.
Then Jesus said, 'Were not ten made clean?
But the other nine, where are they?
Was none of them found to return and give praise to God
except this foreigner?' And he said to him,
'Rise and go on your way; your faith has made you well.'
(Luke 17:11-19)

Reflection
All ten were grateful for what had happened.
But one of them went a step beyond feeling grateful
and reflected on the significance of his experience.

Even when an event is over and in the past
our experience of it can still go on
becoming richer and deeper
when we pause to reflect on its import.

We pause now to reflect on our own ministry,
to become aware of all that we are grateful for,

and to acknowledge the significance
of what we have been given.

Prayer
Response: With all our hearts we bless you, O Lord

We thank God for the enthusiasm we have.
We thank God for staying with us.
We thank God for keeping alive the fire within us.

We thank God for inspiring generous giving in us,
and for the ways in which this has made a difference
to the lives of others.

It is better to give than to receive,
yet it is also in giving that we receive.
We thank God that we have been so blessed in our ministry,
for all we have received when we thought we were only giving.

We thank God for gifts that we have discovered in ourselves.
We bless God for the people we have worked with,
for it is they who have brought out our giftedness.

Ministry means working with others
and all the blessings that brings.
We thank God for opening our hearts to shared ministry
and for learning that strength lies in togetherness.

Glory be ...

Love is our Creed

Scripture
We know that we have passed from death to life
because we love one another.
(1 John 3:14)

A Creed
We believe in the goodness of human life
and we believe in God the creator of all.
We believe in Jesus, God's own beloved;
we believe in the power of his death and resurrection
and that good will triumph over evil.
We believe in God's Spirit, living within and amongst us
uniting us to Jesus and calling us to love.
We believe that we all share this call
and that responding to it we can change the world.
We believe that where love is given and received
we are already experiencing what will be our delight eternally.

Prayers
In these prayers, we think of the elements of the marriage promise,
as reflecting the commitment to love that we are all challenged to,
married or not.

For better or worse
We bless you Lord for your presence in good times and bad;
for good times that have assured us of your kindness,
for bad times when we have experienced your compassion.
We rejoice with all who are happy – in their love and in their children,
in their health and well-being in body and spirit.
We weep with all who weep, for hurt or loss
or conflict or loneliness or despair.
Bless us Lord with a share of your compassion.

For richer or poorer
Some of us know prosperity, some of us know poverty,
and many have known a bit of both.
And we echo the cry of your heart
as we abhor all the inequity and injustice in our world.
Teach us the wisdom to know true value in our prosperity.
Help us see that, though we are poor, we have enough.
But give us also a passion for justice.

In sickness and in health
We bless you, Lord, for health and vitality
and we bless you too for your powerful gentleness
that seeps through us to each other when we are sick or unwell.
Bless us, Lord, with the touch of Jesus.
He touched many when he walked on earth.
Today may we be his hands
and a powerful presence to each other in times of pain.

Blessing
We call upon the Holy Trinity to bless our relationships:
to bless us with unity like that within God,
to bless us with diversity like that within God,
to bless us with intimacy like that within God,
to bless us with creativity like that within God,
to bless us with passion like that within God,
and to draw us ever more deeply,
and to draw us forever, into the life that is God.

Living the Eucharist

In this prayer, we pause over different moments and words from the Mass,
to remind ourselves of how much is contained in what is so familiar to us.

The grace of our Lord Jesus Christ and the love of God
and the fellowship of the Holy Spirit be with you.
Grace, love, fellowship – that each of us may carry this blessed trinity
in our hearts and minds.

Christ have mercy
May all who call on the Lord have a deep realisation
that their lives and existence are bathed in inexhaustible compassion.

This is the word of the Lord
That our hearts may be rich soil, ready and receptive,
where the gospel grows strong roots and bears rich fruit.

Blessed are you, Lord God of all creation
For the goodness of life, for the wonder of the world,
for the miracle of love, for the beauty of the seasons,
for the renewal of hope, we bless you Lord.

Pray that our sacrifice may be acceptable to God the almighty Father
May our lives be a spiritual sacrifice to God,
offered in Jesus' own spirit, with single-minded trust.

Lift up your hearts
May the celebration of the Eucharist be an uplifting experience for all;
may it give us new heart for living.

Do this in memory of me
As we obey the Lord's command, may our remembering keep us in touch
with who he is and who we are.

Let us proclaim the mystery of faith
That our lives may proclaim what our hearts and lips profess;
that gospel joy and hope might radiate out from us.

All glory and honour is yours almighty Father
May all that we do be done for the greater glory of God;
may our lives be a song of praise to God.

As we wait in joyful hope for the coming of our Saviour
May the eyes of our hearts be ever disposed
to see the signs of hope in our midst.

Look not on our sins but on the faith of your church
When our own sinfulness leaves us dispirited,
may our hope be rekindled by the witness of others around us.

Go in peace to love and serve the Lord
May we not hoard what we receive in the Eucharist,
but rather may we realise that in being nourished
we are also sent.

Prayer
For the Eucharist, which is the heart of our lives
and which is the heart of the world,
we give thanks to you, O Lord.

That it may bring forth fruit in our lives
for the transformation of the world,
we pray to you, O Lord.

At the Centre of our Being

The distance between me and God
is the distance between me and myself.

Reflection
The first chirps of the waking day birds
mark the *'point vierge'* of the dawn
under a sky as yet without real light,
a moment of awe and inexpressible innocence,
when the Father in perfect silence
opens their eyes.
They begin to speak to him,
not with fluent song,
but with an awakening question
that is their dawn state,
their state at the *'point vierge'*.
Their condition asks if it is time
for them to 'be'.
He answers 'yes'.
Then, they one by one wake up
and become birds …
The most wonderful moment of the day
is that when creation in its innocence
asks permission to 'be' once again,
as it did on the first morning that ever was.

Pause

At the centre of our being
is a point of nothingness
which is untouched by sin and by illusion,
a point of pure truth,
a point or spark which belongs
entirely to God,

which is never at our disposal,
from which God disposes of our lives,
which is inaccessible to
the fantasies of our own mind
or the brutalities of our own will.
This little point of nothingness
and of absolute poverty
is the pure glory of God in us.
(Thomas Merton)

Quiet

Prayer
God our Creator,
centre of our being,
keep us always in touch with you,
keep us in touch with ourselves.

Jesus our Saviour,
you are the innermost truth about ourselves,
may you be born in us each day.

Spirit of the living God,
spark of new life within us,
keep us faithful through the day
to our dawn state.

Glory be ...

A Prayer for Wisdom

Wisdom is radiant and unfading
and she is easily discerned by those who love her
and is found by those who seek her.
She hastens to make herself known to those who desire her.
(Wisdom 6:12-13)

Scripture
This may be the earliest instance we have of a gathering of Christians,
seeking to discern, through their collective wisdom,
where the Holy Spirit was guiding them.

Now during those days,
when the disciples were increasing in number,
the Hellenists complained against the Hebrews
because their widows were being neglected
in the daily distribution of food.
And the twelve called together the whole community
of the disciples and said, 'It is not right
that we should neglect the word of God
in order to wait on tables. Therefore, friends,
select from among yourselves seven men of good standing,
full of the Spirit and of wisdom,
whom we may appoint to this task,
while we, for our part, will devote ourselves
to prayer and to serving the word.'
What they said pleased the whole community,
and they chose Stephen, a man full of faith and the Holy Spirit,
together with Philip, Prochorus, Nicanor,
Timon, Parmenas, and Nicolaus, a proselyte of Antioch.
They had these men stand before the apostles,
who prayed and laid their hands on them.
(Acts 6:1-6)

Quiet

We open our hearts to the Spirit of the Lord;
may the Spirit bless each of us with openness and wisdom.

Reflection
We bless you, Lord, for your Spirit within and among us.
We bless you for the listening that you nourish in each of us,
enabling us to see beyond our own perspectives,
enabling us to appreciate and understand one another,
enabling us to hear your Spirit speaking to us
through the words and wisdom of one another.
We bless you for blessing us
along the path of discernment.

Prayer
Lord, fill our minds and hearts with your Spirit.
May we be open to whatever your Spirit is saying to us.
May we be open to your Spirit speaking to us
through the words and wisdom of one another.
Heal us from our presumptions and blindspots
lest we be hindered from hearing your word.
Bless us along the path of discernment.

Glory be …

Our Baptism

Scripture
From now on we regard no one
from a human point of view ...
if any one is in Christ,
there is a new creation;
everything old has passed away;
see, everything has become new!
All this is from God,
who reconciled us to himself through Christ
and has given us the ministry of reconciliation ...
So we are ambassadors for Christ,
since God is making his appeal through us.
(2 Cor 5:16-20)

Reflection
With baptism
we become children of God
in his only begotten son, Jesus Christ.
Rising from the waters
of the baptismal font,
every Christian hears again
the voice that was once heard
on the banks of the Jordan river:
'You are my beloved;
with you I am well pleased.'
(John Paul II)

Prayers
Response: Lord, renew in us the Spirit of baptism.

In baptism we are God's beloved.
May all God's people carry the treasure
of this knowledge in their hearts.

May all the baptised appreciate their own giftedness.
May we have the experience of making a difference
in the lives of others,
simply because of who we are.

We are all of us called, in baptism,
to be ambassadors of Christ.
May we dedicate our lives to the coming of his kingdom.

May the grace of baptism be alive in all Christians.
May all feel joy and enthusiasm
as disciples of the risen Jesus.

Together
We pray together in the name in which we are baptised –
in the name of the Father,
the fountain of all life,
in the name of the Son,
the Good News of our salvation,
in the name of the Holy Spirit,
who heals and renews our souls.

Glory be to the Blessed Trinity,
our origin and our destiny.
May we who are baptised into the Trinity
be faithful disciples and enthusiastic companions
on the path of salvation. Amen.

Building Our Parish

Scripture
For we are God's servants, working together;
you are God's field, God's building.
According to the grace of God given to me,
like a skilled master builder I laid a foundation
and someone else is building on it.
Each builder must choose with care how to build on it.
For no one can lay any foundation
other than the one that has been laid;
that foundation is Jesus Christ.

Do you not know that you are God's temple
and that God's Spirit dwells in you?
If anyone destroys God's temple,
God will destroy that person.
For God's temple is holy
and you are that temple.
(1 Corinthians 3:9-11, 16-17)

Come to him, a living stone, though rejected by mortals
yet chosen and precious in God's sight and like living stones,
let yourselves be built into a spiritual house,
to be a holy priesthood, to offer spiritual sacrifices
acceptable to God through Jesus Christ.
(1 Peter 2:4-5)

Prayers of Dedication
We long to be a parish that is fully alive
with you, O Christ, at the centre.
Inspired with this hope we pray.

Response: Spirit of Jesus, you make all things new;
renew our hearts and bind us together.

We dedicate ourselves to building community.
We pray that all parishioners will be concerned for community.
We pray that our parish will be a place of welcome for all,
reaching out to all with the embrace of Christ,
a place where everybody feels included,
young and old, rich and poor.

We dedicate ourselves
to making our celebrations relevant and life-giving.
May our Eucharist be a great celebration of your love, O God.
May it connect with people's lives;
may it speak to our hearts;
may it put words on our hopes;
and may it nourish our spirit from day to day.

We dedicate ourselves
to helping each other grow in faith.
We pray that all God's people in our parish
may come to a deeper understanding of what we believe;
that we may find God in our prayer
and that we may find God in one another;
that our homes may be places of prayer and faith.

We dedicate ourselves
to partnership in the care of our parish.
May priests and parishioners grow in appreciation
of each other's special vocation.
May we learn to share the responsibility
for the care of the people of our parish
and for mapping out our way forward into the future.

Glory be …

Adult Faith

Scripture
When I was a child
I spoke like a child,
I thought like a child
and reasoned like a child.
When I became an adult
I put an end to childish ways.
For now we see in a mirror, dimly,
but then we will see face to face.
Now I know only in part;
then I will know
even as I have been fully known.
(1 Corinthians 13:11-12)

'Let the little children come to me; do not stop them;
for it is to such as these that the kingdom of God belongs.
Truly I tell you, whoever does not receive
the kingdom of God as a little child will never enter it.'
(Mark 10:14-15)

We must no longer be children, tossed to and fro
and blown about by every wind of doctrine, by people's trickery,
by their craftiness in deceitful scheming.
But speaking the truth in love, we must grow up in every way
into him who is the head, into Christ.
(Ephesians 4:14-15)

Reflection
What do these texts suggest to you about adult faith?

Prayers
We are all adults on a journey
out of the past of a child's faith and perceptions
towards a future destiny of divine enlightenment.
Be with us, Lord, as we travel;
urge us to keep moving
onward and outwards and inward.

Even though we grow older
we pray to keep the great qualities of children
we pray for openness and enthusiasm
for a deep trust and confidence in God
for joy in our hearts.

We pray for the faith of an adult,
for mature understanding of what we believe
and a deepening sense of responsibility
for the church and for the world,
for our children and for the future.

Together
Lord, give us a deep appreciation for all your creation,
move us to search and to question,
give us insight and understanding
and the patience to think deeply and to reflect.
May we not stop short with knowledge
but go on to the understanding of heart.
Amen.

Breath Came into Them

Scripture
The hand of the Lord came upon me
and he brought me out by the Spirit of the Lord
and set me down in the middle of a valley; it was full of bones.
He led me all around them; there were very many
lying in the valley, and they were very dry.
He said to me, 'Mortal, can these bones live?'
I answered, 'O Lord God, you know.'
Then he said to me, 'Prophesy to these bones
and say to them, "O dry bones, hear the word of the Lord.
Thus says the Lord God to these bones:
I will cause breath to enter you and you shall live.
I will lay sinews on you and will cause flesh to come upon you
and cover you with skin and put breath in you
and you shall live; and you shall know that I am the Lord".'

So I prophesied as I had been commanded;
and as I prophesied, suddenly there was a noise, a rattling,
and the bones came together, bone to its bone.
I looked and there were sinews on them
and flesh had come upon them and skin had covered them
but there was no breath in them.
Then he said to me, 'Prophesy to the breath,
prophesy, mortal, and say to the breath:
"Thus says the Lord God: Come from the four winds, O breath,
and breathe upon these slain, that they may live".'
I prophesied as he commanded me
and the breath came into them and they lived
and stood on their feet, a vast multitude.

Then he said to me, 'Mortal, these bones are the whole house of Israel.
They say, "Our bones are dried up and our hope is lost;

we are cut off completely." Therefore prophesy and say to them,
"Thus says the Lord God: I am going to open your graves
and bring you up from your graves, O my people,
and I will bring you back to the land of Israel.
And you shall know that I am the Lord when I open your graves
and bring you up from your graves, O my people.
I will put my spirit within you and you shall live
and I will place you on your own soil; then you shall know
that I the Lord have spoken and will act, says the Lord".'
(Ezekiel 37:1-14)

Reflection
Sometimes, Lord, we can offer you successes, hope, progress made.
Other times we have little to offer;
we are dry, lifeless – like these bones –
no inspiration or ideas or vitality –
a sense of failure, or frustration.

Breathe upon us, O Lord,
upon our dry bones.
Make your breath to enter us;
cover our bones with flesh;
bring us from our graves.

Prayer
Response: Put your Spirit within us and we shall live

For each of us, in whatever way we are dry and lifeless,
enliven us with the energy of your Spirit.

For our community of faith, in whatever way our life is dried up,
put your Spirit within us and increase our hope.

For the world and all your people,
that all will feel the breath of your life-giving Spirit.

Glory be ...

Paths

Reflection
Think of a motorway or a highway being built.
The plans are made; the land is bought;
the route is mapped out; the earth is excavated.
The site is alive with cranes and diggers
and noise and activity for months, then years.
Eventually a whole new road is opened.

Think now of a walk in the country.
You leave the road and start across the fields –
perhaps to climb a hill, or reach a river, or arrive at the beach.
In the rough grass you find a path
where the grass has been trodden down
and the ground is firm underfoot.
You look ahead and see that the path is leading where you want to go.

The difference is that here, *the path is made by walking.*
How long has that path been there?
As long as people started to make their way to that hill or river or beach.
As more and more people passed, and as more and more years went by,
the path was made – by walking! So different from the motorway.

In what we do, we do not have a blueprint
that works everything out before we have even started.
In what we do, the path is made by walking. We learn as we go.
We become aware of fellow travellers.
We appreciate those who have started walking ahead of us,
making the path a little clearer.

Scripture
Which of these passages, where the theme of a path occurs, speaks to you about the work of the group at the moment?

Thus says the Lord: stand at the crossroads and look,
and ask for the ancient paths, where the good way lies;
and walk in it, and find rest for your souls.
(Jeremiah 6:16)

You show me the path of life.
(Psalm 16:11)

A voice cries out: in the wilderness prepare the way of the Lord,
make straight in the desert a highway for our God.
(Isaiah 40:3)

Lord, we do not know where you are going;
how can we know the way?
(John 14:5)

Happy are those whose strength is in you,
in whose heart are the highways to Zion.
(Psalm 84:5)

I will instruct you and teach you the way you should go.
(Psalm 32:8)

Was it not you who dried up the sea, the waters of the great deep;
who made the depths of the sea a way for the redeemed to cross over?
(Isaiah 51:10)

You have no trust in the Lord your God
who goes before you on the way,
to show you the route you should take.
(Deuteronomy 1:32-33)

Prayer
Lord, shine light on our path,
put hope in our hearts,
bring fruit to our work.

Bringing People to Jesus

(1)
Scripture
The next day John again was standing with two of his disciples
and as he watched Jesus walk by, he exclaimed,
'Look, here is the Lamb of God!'
The two disciples heard him say this and they followed Jesus.
When Jesus turned and saw them following, he said to them,
'What are you looking for?'
They said to him, 'Rabbi, where are you staying?'
He said to them, 'Come and see.'
They came and saw where he was staying
and remained with him that day.
It was about four o'clock in the afternoon.
One of the two who heard John speak and followed him
was Andrew, Simon Peter's brother.
He first found his brother Simon and said to him,
'We have found the Messiah'. He brought Simon to Jesus,
who looked at him and said, 'You are Simon son of John.
You are to be called Cephas' (which is translated Peter).
(John 1:35-42)

Reflection
Andrew brought his brother Simon to Jesus.
We thank the Lord for all who bring fellow family members to Jesus –
parents and children, children and parents,
brothers and sisters, grandparents, relatives –
through love, through teaching and talking, through witness of life.

(2)

Scripture

Now among those who went up to worship at the festival
were some Greeks. They came to Philip,
who was from Bethsaida in Galilee,
and said to him, 'Sir, we wish to see Jesus.'
Philip went and told Andrew;
then Andrew and Philip went and told Jesus.
Jesus answered them,
'The hour has come for the Son of Man to be glorified.
Very truly I tell you,
unless a grain of wheat falls into the earth and dies,
it remains just a single grain; but if it dies, it bears much fruit.
Those who love their life lose it,
and those who hate their life in this world
will keep it for eternal life.'
(John 12:20-25)

Reflection

Andrew brought strangers from Greece to Jesus,
strangers who wished to see Jesus.
Today more than ever we need the witness of Christians
– their peace and their kindness –
to lead many who have never known Jesus
to want to see him.

Prayer

Lord, you have sent us that others may hear.
Bless us through the intercession of Andrew
who brought other people to you. Amen.

Gifts that Differ

Scripture
Just as a single body
is made up of many members,
each with a different function,
so it is with us;
though we are many,
we are one body in Christ,
all of us linked one to another.
We have a variety of different gifts
and each of us has been graced by the Spirit
in a particular way, for the good of all …
to one is given prophetic vision,
to another, the gift of serving,
to another, teaching,
to another, encouraging,
to another, the gift of a generous spirit,
to another, speaking with wisdom,
to another, the gift of bringing healing,
to another, faith,
to another, helping others,
to another, compassion,
to another, the gift of being cheerful …
So, let us use our gifts, for the good of all;
and we will be building up
the Body of Christ.
(from Romans 12; 1 Corinthians 12; Ephesians 4)

Quiet / Sharing
What are the gifts you bring, to the work and to the group?
Energy? Perception? Co-operative spirit?
Fun? Friendliness? Experience?
Insight? Wisdom? Dedication?
Perseverance? Creativity? Hope?
Imagination? Joy? Affirmation of others?

Think briefly about each other person here.
What are their gifts?
What particular enrichment does each of them bring
to the group and to the work?

Prayers
As we join together in the work of God's kingdom,
may we discover the diverse ways
in which God has gifted each one of us.
May we grow in confidence and in mutual appreciation.
May we bless the Lord.

May God,
who created each one of us with endless variety
teach us to cherish the beauty within,
to appreciate the gifts of others,
and to be thankful for the enrichment
that so much difference brings.

Glory be ...

Hospitality

Scripture
Jesus went out again beside the sea;
the whole crowd gathered around him and he taught them.
As he was walking along, he saw Levi, son of Alphaeus
sitting at the tax-booth and he said to him, 'Follow me.'
And he got up and followed him.
And as he sat at dinner in Levi's house,
many tax-collectors and sinners were also sitting
with Jesus and his disciples
for there were many who followed him.
When the scribes of the Pharisees saw
that he was eating with sinners and tax-collectors,
they said to his disciples,
'Why does he eat with tax-collectors and sinners?'
When Jesus heard this, he said to them,
'Those who are well have no need of a physician,
but those who are sick.
I have come to call not the righteous but sinners.'
(Mark 2:13-17)

Reflection
Imagine being in a strange city,
in a country you were never in before,
where they spoke a language you did not understand.
Imagine walking along the road, unable to read the signs,
seeing people greeting and conversing with one another.
And imagine, in your uncertainty and anxiety,
that you then met somebody you knew,
somebody who lived there but spoke your language,
who invited you back to the warmth of their house.

When Jesus sat at table and ate with tax-collectors and sinners,
it was for them a coming in from the cold.
They were 'outcasts' – they had lost all faith in themselves.
It was as if they were walking in a foreign country, with no way in.
But Jesus who shared table with them spoke their language
and made them insiders instead of strangers.

This same Jesus calls us to conversion.
He calls us to hospitality.
He calls us to reach out and to include.
He calls us to speak to people in their own language.
He calls us to dissolve the feelings people have
of being strangers or outsiders or outcasts.
For these people are God's people.
God speaks and understands their language.
So must we.

Quiet / Sharing
Think of people who may feel not included
or outside our faith community –
people you yourself know –
people you may be only dimly aware of.

Prayer
God our creator and redeemer,
through your son Jesus Christ
you have made us all insiders in your kingdom.
May our imitation and practice
of your inclusive, boundless love
be something real and active.

Advent Prayer

Reflection
Advent – a time of waiting, of expectation, of looking forward.
What am I waiting for, what am I looking forward to?
A few days break at Christmas?
A bit of peace and quiet?
An end to the cold and dark of winter?
Something more, something deeper?
An inner peace ...
a reconciliation ...
a resolution ...
a transformation?
Advent gently reminds us
that we are people who are expecting something.
But maybe I am drifting along, expecting nothing.
Maybe I have nothing to look forward to.
Maybe I am dreading Christmas –
the loneliness, the memories ...

Scripture
The people who walked in darkness have seen a great light;
those who lived in a land of deep darkness –
on them light has shined.
(Isaiah 9:2)

A voice cries out:
'In the wilderness prepare the way of the Lord,
make straight in the desert a highway for our God.'
(Isaiah 40:3)

Quiet Prayer
Winter is darkness, winter is wilderness.
Winter is outside ... winter is inside.
Come to us, Lord, in the wilderness and darkness,
let us see light in our lives.
Fill us with expectation.

Prayers
We pray through Mary, mother of Jesus.

Response: Come, Lord Jesus, come.

As Jesus was born of Mary,
may the life of Christ be born anew in us.

As Mary said 'yes' to the tidings of the Spirit,
may we say 'yes' to what God is doing in our lives.

As Mary waited for the time to come,
may we be filled with expectation of God's coming.

All
We are an advent people,
filled with expectation of God coming amongst us,
to refresh our souls, to renew our world.
Come in Lord, come among us, today and forever.
Amen.

Annunciation

*This prayer reflects on the story of the Annunciation
as a story about hearing and announcing Good News today.*

The angel Gabriel was sent by God to a town ...
God is always communicating with us –
in Nazareth, but also in our town, our place, our parish.
What message of good news might God be sending here today?

'Greetings, favoured one! The Lord is with you ...'
Today, with Mary, we are favoured.
The Lord is with me. The Lord is with us.
This means that I am not alone. This means
that we do not venture forward on our own resources.
We are accompanied.

'Do not be afraid Mary; you have found favour with God ...'
Again and again in the gospels,
we hear these same words from the lips of Jesus –
'Do not be afraid.'
What would we do if we were not afraid?
What is fear holding us from?

She was much perplexed and pondered what sort of greeting this might be ...
Perplexed and pondering – that was Mary; and that is us.
Pondering when perplexed, so that we might hear
what God's Spirit is whispering.

'You will conceive in your womb and bear a son...'
The mystic, Meister Eckhart, once said
that we are all meant to be mothers of God,
because God is always needing to be born.

'He will reign over the house of Jacob forever
and of his kingdom there will be no end ...'
Something has begun that cannot be stopped.
It began in Mary; it has begun in the world;
it has begun in me.

'The Holy Spirit will come upon you ...'
Come Holy Spirit, fill the hearts of the faithful
and kindle in us the fire of your love.
Send forth your Spirit and we will be created
and you will renew the face of the earth.

'Nothing will be impossible to God ...'
'In our human foolishness and short-sightedness
we imagine divine grace to be finite.
But the moment comes when our eyes are opened,
and we see and realise that grace is infinite.
Grace, my friends, demands nothing from us
but that we shall await it with confidence
and acknowledge it in gratitude.'
(Isak Dinesen)

'Here am I, the servant of the Lord;
let it be with me according to your word ...'
May Mary's 'Yes' echo through the church
and through the world,
as God's people say 'Yes' to the possibilities
God sows within us and about us.

Hail Mary ...

Be Opened!

From the Baptism Ritual
The Lord Jesus made the deaf hear and the dumb speak.
May he soon touch your ears to receive his word
and your mouth to proclaim his faith
to the praise and glory of God the Father. Amen.

Scripture
They brought to him a deaf man
who had an impediment in his speech;
and they begged him to lay his hand on him.
He took him aside in private, away from the crowd
and put his fingers into his ears
and he spat and touched his tongue.
Then looking up to heaven, he sighed and said to him,
'Ephphatha,' that is, 'Be opened.'
And immediately his ears were opened,
his tongue was released and he spoke plainly.
Then Jesus ordered them to tell no one;
but the more he ordered them,
the more zealously they proclaimed it.
They were astounded beyond measure, saying,
'He has done everything well;
he even makes the deaf to hear and the mute to speak.'
(Mark 7:32-37)

Prayers
Response: Lord, open our lips, open our ears, open our hearts.

For all baptised Christians –
may each of us come to speak more eloquently
the good news of the gospel, with our lips and with our lives,
with hope-filled speech and hope-filled living.

For all baptised Christians –
may each of us come to listen more intently
and to hear more clearly and to absorb more deeply
the good news of the gospel, the comfort of the gospel,
the joy of the gospel, the challenge of the gospel.

Healing Spirit,
free us from all that blocks us from hearing.
Free us from narrow-mindedness,
from making presumptions, from dismissing others.
Free us from depression and despair,
which prevent us from hearing good news.

Healing Spirit,
free us from all that blocks us from speaking.
Free us from timidity, from lack of courage and confidence.
Free us to realise that in and through our words
you speak wisdom and hope to others.

May each of us speak, not only with our lips,
but also from our heart. May our speech be heart-felt
and may our words always be spoken with love.

May each of us listen, not only with our ears,
but also from our heart. May our listening be heart-filled,
that we may hear with love what the other is saying.

All
Lord Jesus, you made the deaf hear and the dumb speak.
Touch our ears to receive your word.
Touch our mouths to proclaim your faith,
to the praise and glory of God the Father. Amen.

Our Call to Care

For thus says the Lord God:
I myself will search for my sheep and will seek them out.
I will rescue them from all the places
to which they have been scattered
on a day of clouds and thick darkness.
I will feed them with good pasture
and the mountain heights of Israel shall be their pasture;
there they shall lie down in good grazing land.
I myself will be the shepherd of my sheep
and I will make them lie down, says the Lord God.
I will seek the lost and I will bring back the strayed
and I will bind up the injured and I will strengthen the weak.
(Ezekiel 34:11-17)

'I am the good shepherd.
The good shepherd lays down his life for the sheep.
I am the good shepherd.
I know my own and my own know me,
just as the Father knows me and I know the Father.
And I lay down my life for the sheep.'
(John 10:11, 14-15)

Quiet
I become aware of how God cares for me.

Prayers
Response: Lord, teach us to care.

We praise God, our true shepherd,
who, in Jesus, has shown us the depth of his care.

We pause quietly to become aware
of people who are in need in our community,
people in material need or physical need,
people who are emotionally hurt or deprived,
people who are spiritually lost or rootless.

We pause quietly to become aware
of people whose lives are taken up
with caring for others
who are sick or housebound or dependent.

We pause quietly to become aware
of individuals and groups in our parish
who are dedicated to caring
for people in different kinds of need.

God, our true shepherd,
fill our hearts with your care.
Enlarge our hearts to care for those
we find it hard to care for.
Expand our hearts to care for those
whom we are not even aware of.

All
Lord, our shepherd,
may we never want.
May you restore our souls.
May we fear no evil.
May you comfort us.
May goodness and mercy follow us
all the days of our life.

Glory be ...

The Body of Christ

Reflection
This reflection is taken from a homily of St Augustine, from around 400 AD entitled 'To the Newly Baptised concerning the Eucharist'. New (adult) Christians went through an elaborate preparation, but it was only when they had been baptised that they were initiated into the mystery of the Eucharist.

What you see is the bread and the chalice –
this is what your eyes tell you.
But what your faith needs to be informed of –
the bread is the body of Christ, the chalice is his blood.
This is why these things are called sacraments,
because in them one thing is seen, but another is understood.

If you wish to understand the body of Christ,
listen to what the apostle says to the believers,
'You are the body of Christ and his members.'
If, therefore, you are the body of Christ and his members,
it is your own mystery that has been placed
on the table of the Lord.
It is your own mystery that you receive.

To this which you are you respond 'Amen'
and in responding, you accept it.
What you hear is 'the Body of Christ'
and to this you respond 'Amen'.
So, be a member of Christ's body,
that your Amen may be true.

Let us listen to the apostle, who says in the same place,
'there is one bread, so we who are many are one body.'
'One bread' – what is this one bread?
'We who are many are one body.'

Remember that bread is not made from one grain but from many.
When you were being exorcised,
it was as if you had been ground down.
When you were baptised it is as if you were moistened.
When you accepted the fire of the Holy Spirit,
it is as if you had been baked.
Be what you see and accept what you are.

This the apostle said of the bread;
yet it tells us too the meaning of the chalice.
For remember how wine is made.
Many grapes hang from the vine, but all the juice flows into one.
And that is what Jesus Christ means to us.
He wants us to belong in him, to pour into him as one.
It is the mystery of our peace and unity
which he consecrates on his table.

Prayer
Christ has no body now on earth but yours;
he has no hands on earth but yours;
he has no feet on earth but yours.
It is your eyes through which
his compassion is to look out upon the world.
It is your feet with which
he is to go about doing good.
It is your hands with which
he is to bless people now.
Christ has no body now on earth but yours.
(attributed to Teresa of Avila)

All
Grant that we who are nourished by his body and blood
may be filled with his Holy Spirit
and become one body, one spirit in Christ.

Glory be …

Be Seen and Unseen

Scripture
In the sermon on the mount, Jesus speaks of how we should be visible:
'You are the light of the world.
A city built on a hill cannot be hid.
No one after lighting a lamp puts it under the bushel basket
but on the lampstand, and it gives light to all in the house.
In the same way, let your light shine before others
so that they may see your good works
and give glory to your Father in heaven.'
(Matthew 5:14-16)

In the same sermon Jesus also says we should be unseen:
'When you give alms, do not let your left hand know
what your right hand is doing
so that your alms may be done in secret …
Whenever you pray, go into your room and shut the door
and pray to your Father who is in secret …
When you fast, put oil on your head and wash your face,
so that your fasting may be seen not by others
but by your Father who is in secret …'
(Matthew 6:3-4, 6, 17-18)

Reflection
Lord, you call us to be seen and unseen –
how can that be?

You call us to be *seen* by others, in the good we do.
Is it because we have so much to give,
because you have gifted us so,
and our giftedness is destined to be for the enrichment of others?

Yet you also call us to be *unseen* in the good we do.
Is that because we easily become proud,
because our inclinations face inwards as well as outwards,
and we can so easily do good to fulfil our own needs?

You call us to be *visible* as witnesses to your gospel.
Is it because good news received cannot be kept to ourselves,
that it is unthinkable that it would not be shared in return?
Is it because it is only through sharing good news
that we receive it fully into our hearts?
Is it because it is only through people like us
that the good news of the kingdom will be heard in the world?

You call us to be *unseen* as witnesses to your gospel.
Is it because the spotlight could so easily be focused on us,
that people might see us and not you?
Is it because we could become complacent,
basking in our achievements,
rather than drawn out of ourselves by your mission?

Lord, this is a hard balance to achieve!

Prayers
Lord, amidst all our mixed motives, give us a pure heart.
We want to learn to do what is good and right for its own sake,
out of a passion for goodness,
with the spotlight on goodness and not on ourselves.

Lord, give us a bold heart.
We want to give from what we have received
and to witness to you in our world.

Lord, teach us to be seen and unseen.
May we be both humble and courageous.
May we be self-effacing and not self-seeking.
May your glory shine forth in our lives.

Glory be...

Being Ministered to

Scripture
While he was at Bethany in the house of Simon the leper,
as he sat at the table, a woman came with an alabaster jar
of very costly ointment of nard and she broke open the jar
and poured the ointment on his head.
(Mark 14:3)

Jesus came to Bethany, the home of Lazarus
whom he had raised from the dead.
There they gave a dinner for him. Martha served
and Lazarus was one of those at the table with him.
Mary took a pound of costly perfume made of pure nard,
anointed Jesus' feet and wiped them with her hair.
The house was filled with the fragrance of the perfume.
(John 12:1-3)

One of the Pharisees asked Jesus to eat with him
and he went into the Pharisee's house and took his place at the table.
And a woman in the city who was a sinner,
having learned that he was eating in the Pharisee's house,
brought an alabaster jar of ointment.
She stood behind him at his feet, weeping,
and began to bathe his feet with her tears and to dry them with her hair.
Then she continued kissing his feet and anointing them with the ointment.
(Luke 7:36-38)

Reflection
When, on the last night of his life, Jesus offered his friends a gesture
that would express his heart and his life, he washed the feet of Peter.
It is speculative, but not inconceivable that the origin of the idea
lay in the experience Jesus had of having his own feet washed.

We are used to thinking of the 'ministry of Jesus',
of his life on earth as a pure pattern of giving.
We are not used to thinking of him as receiving ministry.
We are used to thinking of him as gracing others; not as being graced.
We are used to thinking of him as responding to need; not as needing.

Today, many people engaged in the exercise of care
can be generous in their serving, but neglectful of their own needs.
They can even find it difficult to allow themselves to be cared for.
It is said that it is better to give than to receive,
but it can be harder to receive than to give!

Yet some of our deepest insights into the meaning of ministry
come from our experience of receiving ministry.
Perhaps that is how it was with Jesus.

Prayers
We came into being because of God's desire to love us.
May each day of our lives see us graciously allowing God to love us.

May we learn more and more to enjoy being loved and cared for.
May the awareness of being loved brighten up our lives.

May pride or superiority or any other obstacle not stand in the way
of allowing others to minister to us.

May the ministry we receive from others teach us how to minister in turn.
May the care we receive teach us how to care.
May the love of others release the love in our hearts.

May the life of our community be filled with the fragrance of ministry.
May it be the aroma of the life of the Trinity,
an endless giving and receiving of life.

Glory be ...

The Fruits of the Spirit

Scripture
'The fruit of the Spirit is love, joy, peace, patience, kindness,
generosity, faithfulness, gentleness and self-control.'
(Galatians 5:22)

Reflection
Jesus told us, 'The Holy Spirit, whom the Father will send in my name,
will teach you everything and remind you of all that I have said to you'.
The Spirit is in us and part of us, bringing to life in us what Jesus said and
did. The fruits of the Spirit are the values of Jesus pervading our lives.

As we remember Jesus' words, we might ask ourselves:
what fruit of the Spirit do I most wish for in my life?

Prayers
Response: May the Spirit of Jesus bear fruit in our lives.

LOVE
After washing Peter's feet, Jesus said, 'This is my commandment,
that you love one another as I have loved you.'
We pray for a loving heart.

JOY
Jesus said, 'Rejoice that your names are written in heaven.'
We pray for a spirit of joy.

PEACE
'Jesus came and stood among them and said, Peace be with you.'
We pray for peace in our hearts.

PATIENCE
Jesus said, 'The kingdom of God is as if someone would scatter seed on the
ground, and would sleep and rise night and day, and the seed would sprout
and grow, he does not know how.'
We pray for patient trust.

KINDNESS
Jesus said, 'You will be children of the Most High;
for he is kind to the ungrateful and the wicked.
Be merciful, just as your Father is merciful.'
We pray to be kind in our thoughts, words and actions.

GENEROSITY
'He said, Truly I tell you, this poor widow has put in more than all of them;
for all of them have contributed out of their abundance,
but she out of her poverty has put in all she had to live on.'
We pray that we may learn to give more and more of ourselves.

FAITHFULNESS
At the last supper, Jesus said to his disciples,
'You are those who have stood by me in my trials.'
We pray that we may be faithful disciples.

GENTLENESS
Jesus said, 'Blessed are the gentle, for they will inherit the earth.'
We pray that we may be gentle with each person and each created thing.

SELF-CONTROL
Jesus said, 'For out of the heart come evil intentions,
murder, adultery, fornication, theft, false witness, slander.
These are what defile a person.'
We pray for self-control, that evil may not spread from our hearts.

Together
The love of God flowing free
The love of God flow out through me.
The peace of God flowing free
The peace of God flow out through me.
The life of God flowing free
The life of God flow out through me.

Meditation – for an Evening Meeting

A meditation looking back over the day.
As you relax and get comfortable, make yourself ready to travel back
over the journey from this morning when you awoke until now.

When I awoke …
the sleep in my eyes, the thoughts in my head, the water on my face …
when was the first time I looked out the window …
the first time I looked in the mirror …
the first person I spoke with …
the prayer I said this morning …

And the time from then until the middle of the day,
what the morning contained …
the tasks that occupied me …
conversations I had …
trips I made …
people's faces …

And then, lunchtime …
what did I choose to eat …
was I alone, who was I with …
what was it like …

And the afternoon time …
the things I did …
the places I went …
the people I was with …
the tiredness … satisfaction … disappointment …

Right up until the evening meal, perhaps coming home,
perhaps a wash … that special time,
the first journey of the day over, the second beginning …

From where I am now, looking back down the journey of the day ...
what feelings were in my heart at different times ...
boredom, anger, happiness, worry, satisfaction, love ...

And visiting the memory of my eyes,
all that my eyes took in without noticing ...
unlocking the memory of my eyes this day ...
what did my eyes see ...
which I now store properly, to return to afterwards ...

During this day, what blessings did I receive ...
what graces did I bestow ...
where was God ...

And now as I conclude this meditation ...
my hopes for the evening of this day, for this gathering ...

Prayer
Lord, you go before us at every moment of the day.
You are in every person we meet
and in every experience we have.
We are always catching up with you in our lives,
always finding you had been there,
not realising it at the time.

Expand and enrich our awareness,
our capacity for attending to your presence
and recognising your grace.
Amen.

A Listening Heart

SCRIPTURE
Then the Lord said,
'I have observed the misery of my people who are in Egypt;
I have heard their cry on account of their taskmasters.
Indeed, I know their sufferings
and I have come down to deliver them from the Egyptians
and to bring them up out of that land to a good and broad land,
a land flowing with milk and honey.'
(Exodus 3:7-8)

Meditation
Our God is a listening God
who hears the cry of the poor,
who bends down and comes to our aid.

Our God calls on each of us to become
a listening heart, attentive to one another
with something of God's own listening heart ...

Meditate now on the way in which being listened to
is such a dignifying experience.
To be listened to is to feel important.

Think of the special people in your life
who see and notice and understand you;
give thanks to the listening God
who has sent these 'angels' to you.

Think of times you were dignified by being listened to;
think of times when the opposite happened.

Thank God that you are so important
and pray that you may confer the same dignity on others
by your listening to them.

Pray that you may be able to empty yourself
to become available,
to become a listening heart.

Prayer
We bless you, O God,
for how dignified we feel when somebody listens to us.
We thank you, O God,
for times when we have blessed others with a listening ear.
We praise you, O God,
for listening to the cries of your people.

Through our ministry and the ministry of many others,
make us a listening community
where each person is noticed,
where each voice is heard,
where each gift is appreciated,
where each one comes to know that you are a listening God.

Bless our group with the gift of listening.
May we listen and hear what each other is saying.
May we step into each other's shoes and see things from there.
May we hear the wisdom of the Spirit in each other's voices.

Glory be ...

Collaboration then and now

Scripture
The next day Moses sat as judge for the people,
while the people stood around him from morning until evening.
When Moses' father-in-law saw all that he was doing for the people,
he said, 'What is this that you are doing for the people?
Why do you sit alone, while all the people stand around you
from morning until evening?'
The task is too heavy for you; you cannot do it alone.
Look for able men among all the people.
Let them bring every important case to you,
but decide every minor case themselves.
So it will be easier for you and they will bear the burden with you.
(Exodus 18:13-14, 18, 21-22)

Way back in the origins of our faith,
we see the spirit of partnership beginning to stir.
We learn that the task is too much for any one of us.
We see that nothing is too burdensome if we bear it together.

Scripture
Moses said to the Lord, 'Why have you treated your servant so badly?
Why have I not found favour in your sight,
that you lay the burden of all this people on me?
Did I conceive all this people?
Where am I to get meat to give to all this people?
For they come weeping to me and say, 'Give us meat to eat.'
I am not able to carry all this people alone, for they are too heavy for me' ...
So the Lord said to Moses, 'Gather for me seventy of the elders of Israel ...
and I will take some of the spirit that is on you and put it on them;
and they shall bear the burden of the people along with you
so that you will not bear it all by yourself.'
(Numbers 11:11-14, 16-17)

We pray for our priests who have been carrying a weight for the sake of all of us.
We bless them for their great-hearted giving.
We ask God to bless us all as we learn to share together in the work of the Spirit.

Scripture
After this the Lord appointed seventy others
and sent them on ahead of him in pairs
to every town and place where he himself intended to go.
He said to them, 'The harvest is plentiful, but the labourers are few;
therefore ask the Lord of the harvest to send labourers into his harvest.
(Luke 10:1-2)

May each baptised, confirmed Christian come to see that they are called,
each one called by name, to co-operate together in the mission of Jesus.

Reflection
The Lord himself renews his invitation to all the lay faithful
to come closer to him every day,
and with the recognition that what is his is also their own,
they ought to associate themselves with him
in his saving mission.
Once again he sends them into every town and place
where he himself is to come.
(John Paul II)

Prayer
Spirit of the risen Jesus, guide the church at this new moment
in the unfolding of God's kingdom among us.
In the experience of collaboration in ministry,
you reveal to us a truth about who we are.
Inspire us to trust in this grace,
allay our fears and refresh our energy,
as we praise you for increasing our hope.

Glory be...

For Widowed and Separated People

Prayer for People who are Widowed

We belong to a tradition going back to the people of Israel
and continuing in the Christian community of the New Testament,
a tradition that commits itself to having a particular regard
for the orphan and the widow in their defencelessness.

Faithful to that tradition, we pray today
for all who are widowed amongst us,
who live in this tender and delicate state,
bearing the pain of absence and silence,
carrying a loss that is irreplaceable,
no matter what kind words we speak.

May boundless Compassion be with all who are widowed,
may they sense the touch of infinite Compassion.

We hope that the widowed women and men among us
will be able to go on witnessing
to the best in the one whom they have loved,
to the qualities they cherished and admired.
By this they testify that the union continues
through this temporary absence.

We give thanks for the treasures that are carried in memories.
We give thanks for having experienced love in life,
for having been loved and having been able to love to return,
for touching thereby upon the infinite mystery of love.

May this treasure never lose its radiance
during the time of absence,
but may it bring courage to go on loving
and bring peace within the silence.

O God, you are closer to us than our innermost selves,
you have sewn our lives together in the cradle of your heart.

Prayer for People who are Separated

In prayer we embrace all God's people who, having married,
are now separated – women and men;
those who separated early in their marriage
and those who separated later;
those who feel themselves the victims of separation
and those who blame themselves;
those whose separating was relatively calm,
and those for whom it was a bitter and violent experience.

It is our faith that God graces marriage with an infinite beauty.
But it is also our faith that God's heart grieves
for all who have been disappointed in life.
We believe that God feels with and for all
whose experience didn't match up to their dream.

We too feel God's feelings
and we pray for our sisters and brothers who are separated.
May Jesus, whose touch healed so many and so powerfully
when he walked on earth, touch and heal you.

Where you feel a failure, may he ease your recrimination;
Where you feel disappointment, may he reassure your spirit;
Where you feel resentful, may he help any evil in your heart to die;
Where you feel victimised, may he be your vindication;
Where you feel guilty, may he rejoice in your repentance.

We especially pray for a bright future for separated people,
lest they be imprisoned in memories of pain.
We pray that they rediscover love.
May all who have been disappointed by marriage
find again the vocation to love and the experience of love
that is at the heart of being human for all of us.

Reaching Out and Reaching In

Reflection
With every creature, Meister Eckhart says,
according to the nobility of its nature,
the more it indwells in itself, the more it gives itself out.
A metaphor may clarify his meaning.
Imagine some object, a book,
leaning out over the edge of a table.
There comes a moment when it will overbalance
if it leans any further.
Its reaching out must be balanced by its reaching in.

If I have only a shallow inreach – interiority – in my life,
then my outreach to others will be full of hazards.
The way to reach further out is to reach further in.
If I am reluctant to live from the full interiority of my spirit,
then I will have little to bring to others,
no matter how much I involve myself in their lives.
While, on the other hand, there are people who can enter
another's life for half-an-hour and leave it transformed.

I think of these people as having
some of the depth and power that Jesus had.
This human experience of inreach and outreach is a chink
through which we can glimpse the mystery of God's life.
It is because God has fathomless inner life
that God can reach so far out in creation.

All creatures, then, have a double depth.
Their being shows God's outreach to us,
and we feel the fascination of this.
But creatures also manifest God's inner life,
and this should fascinate us no less.

The interiority of God is translated into human reality in Jesus.
He is God reaching out to us from inexhaustible depths.
In the words of Leo the Great,
'he is the hand of God's mercy stretched out to us.'
(Donagh O'Shea)

Prayers
Response: May your life be made visible in us, O Lord.

'You cannot feed the world from an empty dish.'
Reaching out comes from reaching in.
So, may we take time to reach in more profoundly.
May we hear the gospel again, as if for the first time.
May we recover our initial sense of amazement.
In that energy, may we reach out.

'It is in giving that we receive.'
Our outreach also deepens our inreach.
So, may we be open and ready for learning.
May we listen intently to those to whom we reach out.
May we allow them to teach us
the truth and the mystery of the gospel.

All
Spirit of the living God, enrich us in our double depth.
Inspire us to reach out with courage and with openness.
Inspire us to reach in with humility and expectation.
May our reaching out and reaching in
be a participation in the coming of the kingdom
unveiled among us by Jesus the Lord. Amen.

Evangelisation

Scripture
Now the apostles and the believers who were in Judea
heard that the Gentiles had also accepted the word of God.
So when Peter went up to Jerusalem,
the circumcised believers criticised him, saying,
'Why did you go to uncircumcised men and eat with them?'
Then Peter began to explain it to them, step by step, saying:

'I was in the city of Joppa praying and in a trance I saw a vision.
There was something like a large sheet coming down from heaven,
being lowered by its four corners; and it came close to me.
As I looked at it closely I saw four-footed animals,
beasts of prey, reptiles and birds of the air.
I also heard a voice saying to me, "Get up, Peter; kill and eat."
But I replied, "By no means, Lord;
for nothing profane or unclean has ever entered my mouth".'

But a second time the voice answered from heaven:
"What God has made clean you must not call profane."
This happened three times; then everything was pulled up again to heaven.
At that very moment three men, sent to me from Caesarea,
arrived at the house where we were.
The Spirit told me to go with them
and not to make a distinction between them and us.

These six brothers also accompanied me
and we entered the man's [Cornelius] house.
He told us how he had seen the angel standing in his house
and saying, "Send to Joppa and bring Simon who is called Peter;
he will give you a message by which you
and your entire household will be saved."
As I began to speak, the Holy Spirit fell upon them,

just as it had on us at the beginning.
And I remembered the word of the Lord, how he had said,
"John baptised with water, but you will be baptised with the Holy Spirit."
If then God gave them the same gift that he gave to us
when we believed in the Lord Jesus Christ,
who was I that I could hinder God?'

When they heard this they were silenced.
And they praised God, saying, 'Then God has given
even to the Gentiles the repentance that leads to life.'
(Acts 11:1-18)

Reflection / Sharing
In this story there were two conversions –
the conversion of Cornelius and the conversion of Peter.
Cornelius' conversion was to the gospel,
while Peter was already a believer.
But Peter had presumed that God was a God of the Jews.
He learned to see that God's Spirit blows where it wills,
that it is bigger than our categories
and always at work in surprising new ways.

Prayers
Lord, forgive us for the ways in which we try to control your Spirit,
to reduce the actions of your Spirit to the limits of our own vision.

Lord, expand the vision of our hearts; make us open
to delight in the surprising ways your Spirit acts in our world.

May we as a church be open to the world around us.
May we see the world as the arena of your Spirit's activity.

In reaching out to others, may we always remember to honour them,
for the Spirit is already alive in their lives, long before we meet them.

Glory be ...

Setting Out

Scripture
By faith Abraham obeyed
when he was called to set out for a place
that he was to receive as an inheritance;
and he set out, not knowing
where he was going.
(Hebrews 11:8)

Reflection
The task is huge.
We are to bring the gospel into a new century,
to face challenges we have not begun to imagine,
to respond to opportunities we have not anticipated,
with the great variety of gifts
which we do not fully realise we have.
(Donal Murray)

Prayers
As we venture forward,
in expectation and in apprehension,
we pray for your blessing, O Lord,
and for the enthusing power of your Spirit ...

Response: Bless us, O Lord

Bless us, O Lord, with hope.
Teach us to see the signs of hope in our midst
and to approach our task in a spirit of hope and confidence.

Bless us, O Lord, with listening.
Your Spirit works through each of us and speaks through each of us.
Teach us to listen to one another with an open and generous disposition.

Bless us, O Lord, with appreciation.
As a group, we are rich with a variety of gifts.
Teach us to see what is positive in each other
and to welcome and prize it as a gift from you.

Bless us, O Lord, with perseverance.
The seeds we are sowing grow slowly;
teach us to be patient and to trust.

Bless us, O Lord, with joy.
Teach us to enjoy being together and working together.

Together
God of Blessings,
may your blessing of life-made-more-liveable
touch and enrich the lives of many.

Creator God,
may we see something of your creativity
in the creative talents to be revealed in our group.

God of Love,
may a spirit of dedicated service be present here,
making real your loving and self-giving care for all.

God of Beauty,
may we see in our work a reflection
of your beauty, variety, brightness and colour;
may this fill us with wonder and awe,
may it raise our hearts and spirits to you.

Good God, circle us with your love,
embrace *within* all that is good and wholesome and beneficial,
keep *without* all that is evil and harmful and destructive.

The Kingdom

Reflection: 'The Kingdom'
It's a long way off but inside it
There are quite different things going on:
Festivals at which a poor man
Is king and the consumptive is
Healed; mirrors in which the blind look
At themselves and love looks at them
Back; and industry is for mending
The bent bones and the minds fractured
By life. It's a long way off, but to get
There takes no time and admission
Is free, if you will purge yourself
Of desire, and present yourself with
Your need only and the simple offering
Of your faith, green as a leaf.
(R. S. Thomas)

Quiet / Sharing
What God's 'kingdom' or 'reign' means to me.

Scripture
Now after John was arrested,
Jesus came to Galilee,
proclaiming the good news of God and saying,
'The time is fulfilled
and the kingdom of God has come near;
repent and believe in the good news.'
(Mark 1:14-15)

Prayers
Response: Your Kingdom Come

As we listen to these first words of Jesus,
may his spirit of good news fill our hearts.

As we listen to these first words of Jesus,
may his vision of God's reign permeate our minds.

As we listen to these first words of Jesus,
may his expectation of God's reign inspire our living.

Together
Father, breathe your Spirit
upon your people who do your work.
Grace us, we pray, with
a new sense of your mystery,
a new experience of your presence,
a new commitment to your gospel,
a new dedication to your kingdom.
May your Spirit be our inspiration
and may our work contribute to
the coming of your reign.
Amen.

A Prayer for Parish Visitation

Scripture
We listen to what Jesus said to those he sent visiting,
to hear what he is saying to us.

After this the Lord appointed seventy others and sent them on
ahead of him in pairs to every town and place
where he himself intended to go.
He said to them, 'The harvest is plentiful, but the labourers are few;
therefore ask the Lord of the harvest to send labourers into his harvest.
Go on your way. See, I am sending you out
like lambs into the midst of wolves.
Carry no purse, no bag, no sandals; and greet no one on the road.
Whatever house you enter, first say, 'Peace to this house!'
And if anyone is there who shares in peace,
your peace will rest on that person;
but if not, it will return to you. Remain in the same house,
eating and drinking whatever they provide,
for the labourer deserves to be paid.
Do not move about from house to house.
Whenever you enter a town and its people welcome you,
eat what is set before you; cure the sick who are there and say to them,
'The kingdom of God has come near to you.'
But whenever you enter a town and they do not welcome you,
go out into its streets and say,
'Even the dust of your town that clings to our feet,
we wipe off in protest against you. Yet know this:
the kingdom of God has come near.' I tell you, on that day
it will be more tolerable for Sodom than for that town.'
(Luke 10:1-12)

Prayers
Response: Blessed be Jesus, in whom God's kingdom has come near to us.

He sent them on ahead of him in pairs
We feel apprehensive about visiting the homes of the parish.
But we know that strength comes from togetherness.
We are thankful to have the support of each other in this venture.

Ask the Lord of the harvest to send labourers into his harvest
This used to be mean just priests and nuns and brothers.
But now we know that all of us – men and women, younger and older,
richer and poorer – are called to do this work together.

I am sending you out like lambs in the midst of wolves
It's good to know that Jesus knows what it might be like!
Jesus knows that we might be like lambs amidst wolves,
but still he sends us. Surely that means that it will be alright.

Carry no purse, no bag, no sandals
This reminds us that what we bring above all is ourselves –
and your Spirit, O Lord, which you promise to us.
We pray that people may see you in us, just as we see you in them.

First say, 'peace to this house'
We know that, when we visit, our brief doorstep encounters
are more than just casual meetings. May they bring to many people
a real inner sense of your peace, O Lord.

Cure the sick who are there
This sounds like too much for us – but perhaps somewhere along the way,
our visiting might bring a moment of healing into somebody's life –
a moment when something is set right or made whole.

It will be more tolerable for Sodom
You remind us, Lord, of the sin of inhospitality committed long ago
by the people of Sodom. May our visits be a time of hospitality.
Just as we hope to be welcomed wherever we go, so also we hope
that people will find in us a sense of welcome from the parish.

Glory be …

Pastoral Planning

Reflection
We must set about drawing up
an effective post-Jubilee pastoral plan.
It is not a matter of inventing a 'new programme'.
The programme already exists –
it is the plan found in the gospel;
it has its centre in Christ himself.
But it must be translated into pastoral initiatives
adapted to the circumstances of each community.
The Jubilee has given us an extraordinary opportunity.
But now it is no longer an immediate goal that we face,
but the larger and more demanding challenge
of normal pastoral activity.
It is in the local churches
that the specific features of a detailed pastoral plan
can be identified –
goals and methods,
formation and enrichment of the people involved,
the search for the necessary resources –
which will enable the proclamation of Christ
to reach people,
mould communities,
and have a deep and incisive influence
in bringing gospel values to bear in society and culture.
(John Paul II)

Prayer
Response: May the good news of the gospel be heard in the world.

We are called to bring the gospel into a new millennium.
May we not be frightened by the awesomeness of the task.
Rather, may we be excited by the prospect of sharing good news.

We cannot foresee everything.
We will face challenges that we had not expected.
May our spirit of hope sustain us.
May our togetherness encourage us.

We cannot foresee everything.
We will come across opportunities that will surprise us.
May our openness enable us to appreciate those occasions
and to make the most of them.

As we venture forward, we do so with a great variety of gifts,
many of which we do not realise we have –
gifts in ourselves and gifts throughout our community.
May we learn to affirm and encourage the giftedness in each other.
May we learn to recognise and appreciate
the many manifestations of God's Spirit in people.

Our planning is a participation in God's plan for us.
May our faith and prayer allow us to be shaped by the Spirit
in our vision and in our action.

Glory be...

Resurrection

*'I beseech you, be transformed. Resolve to know that in you
there is a capacity to be transformed.' (Origen)*

Scripture
Then Jesus, again greatly disturbed, came to the tomb.
It was a cave and a stone was lying against it.
Jesus said, 'Take away the stone.'
When he had said this, he cried with a loud voice,
'Lazarus, come out!' The dead man came out,
his hands and feet bound with strips of cloth
and his face wrapped in a cloth.
Jesus said to them, 'Unbind him and let him go.'
(John 11:38-39, 43-44)

Reflection
Albert Camus wrote, 'In the midst of winter I finally learned
that there was in me an invincible summer.'
That is the resurrection voice,
calling us from despair and all its defeats
to the possibility of transformation,
and the transformation begins in our hearts, in our attitudes.

Resurrection is refusing to be imprisoned by history and its long hatreds;
it is the determination to take the first step out of the tomb.
Resurrection is refusing to be gripped for ever by the fingers of winter,
whatever our winter may be.

It may be a personal circumstance that immobilises us,
or a social evil that confronts us;
whatever it is, we simply refuse to accept it,
because the logic of Resurrection calls us to action.
If we say we believe in the Resurrection, the claim only has meaning
if we believe in the possibility of transformed lives,

transformed attitudes
and transformed societies.
The payoff comes in the action that accompanies our belief;
the payoff is the proof of the belief.
So I end with what may appear to be a paradox:
I believe in the Resurrection, the Christ Resurrection,
because I see resurrections now,
see stones rolled away and new possibilities rising from old attitudes.
And my belief in resurrection means that I must commit myself
to the possibility of transformation and, however feeble I feel,
take the first faltering step toward personal change.

More importantly, it means joining with others to bring new life
to human communities that are still held in the grip of winter.
Engaging in that exhilarating action is believing in the Resurrection.
(Richard Holloway)

Quiet / Sharing
Where do I see stones being rolled away?
Where do I see life emerging?

Prayer
We pray for your transforming Resurrection Spirit, O Lord,
We pray for transformation in our hearts and in our attitudes;
for transformed lives; for transformed relationships;
for transformed community; for a transformation of society
and the transformation of the world.
We pray that all would be transformed
according to the pattern of your kingdom, your reign,
brought into being through Jesus your Son. Amen.

Be Still and Know

Scripture
God is our refuge and strength,
a very present help in trouble.
Therefore, we will not fear,
though the earth should change,
though the mountains shake in the heart of the sea;
though its waters roar and foam,
though the mountains tremble with its tumult.
The nations are in an uproar, the kingdoms totter;
he utters his voice, the earth melts.
'Be still, and know that I am God!
I am exalted among the nations.
I am exalted in the earth.'
(Psalm 46:1-3, 6, 10)

On that day, when evening had come, he said to them,
'Let us go across to the other side.'
And leaving he crowd behind,
they took him with them in the boat, just as he was.
Other boats were with him.
A great windstorm arose and the waves beat into the boat,
so that the boat was already being swamped.
But he was in the stern, asleep on the cushion;
and they woke him up and said to him,
'Teacher, do you not care that we are perishing?'
He woke up and rebuked the wind and said to the sea,
'Peace! Be still!'
Then the wind ceased and there was a dead calm.
He said to them, 'Why are you afraid? Have you still no faith?'
And they were filled with great awe and said to one another,
'Who then is this, that even the wind and the sea obey him?'
(Mark 4:35-41)

Reflection
The earth melts. It is silent. It is still. It knows who is God.
Let us be silent and still.
Let us know who is who – that God is God,
supreme over all creation,
over every fear and dread and alarm,
over every panic and terror of our hearts.

God shouts, 'Be still and know!'
I think of my fear;
I think of whatever possesses me,
whatever is driving or dominating me,
and I pray:
may God be the supreme power in my life.

God shouts, 'Be still and know!'
I think of our world,
of the forces and fear that dominate it,
of the obsessions and illusions that control it,
and I pray:
may God be the supreme power in our world.

Quiet

Together
Glory be to God
whose power working among us
is able to accomplish
far more than we could ever ask or imagine.
Glory be the Father and to the Son
and to the Holy Spirit,
as it was in the beginning, is now,
and ever shall be, world without end. Amen.

What is a Parish for?

The parish is not principally a structure,
a territory, or a building,
but rather the family of God,
a fellowship afire with a unifying Spirit,
a familial and welcoming home,
the community of the faithful.
It is a Eucharistic community,
a people well suited for celebrating the Eucharist

The parish is the church
situated in the neighbourhoods of humanity.
Its way is to be deeply inserted in human society
and intimately bound up with people's aspirations
and with the dramatic events of their lives.

Life today can be disintegrated and dehumanised.
The individual may be lost or disoriented.
But there always remains in the human heart
the desire to experience and cultivate
caring and personal relationships.

The parish can respond to this desire
when its people participate
in its essential mission and calling
which is to be a place in the world
for the community of believers to gather together,
to be a house of welcome to all
and a place of service to all –
to be 'the village fountain'
to which all would have recourse in their thirst.
(John Paul II)

Quiet / Sharing
Repeat a word or phrase that stays with you from the reflection.
Speak about it if you wish.

Prayer
God of our Lord Jesus Christ,
as we share together in the life of our parish family,
we ask you:

Lead us onwards,
on the journey of discovering your dream for us;

Lead us outwards,
in love and solidarity, cherishing each other and every other;

Lead us upwards,
to experience more intensely your inexpressible life;

Lead us inwards,
deeper into the mystery of what you have created us to be.

Glory be …

Service

Scripture
Jesus called them and said to them,
'You know that among the Gentiles
those whom they recognise as their rulers lord it over them
and their great ones are tyrants over them.
But it is not so among you;
but whoever wishes to become great among you must be your servant,
and whoever wishes to be first among you must be slave of all.
For the Son of Man came not to be served but to serve
and to give his life a ransom for many
(Mark 10:42-45)

Be of the same mind, having the same love,
being in full accord and of one mind.
Do nothing from selfish ambition or conceit,
but in humility regard others as better than yourselves.
Let each of you look not to your own interests
but to the interests of others.
Let the same mind be in you that was in Christ Jesus
who, though he was in the form of God,
did not regard equality with God
as something to be exploited,
but emptied himself, taking the form of a slave.
(Philippians 2:2-7)

Who among you would say to your slave
who has just come in from ploughing
or tending sheep in the field,
'Come here at once and take your place at the table'?
Would you not rather say to him,
'Prepare supper for me, put on your apron
and serve me while I eat and drink;

86

later you may eat and drink'?
Do you thank the slave for doing what was commanded?
So you also, when you have done all that you
were ordered to do, say, 'We are worthless slaves;
we have done only what we ought to have done!'
(Luke 17:7-10)

Quiet / Sharing
What does it mean to you, to describe our work as 'service'?

Prayer
Response: May Jesus' spirit of service fill our hearts and our work.

In a spirit of service, may we grow in reverence and respect
for all God's people.

In our relationship to those we minister with,
may the spirit of service be to the fore.
May we resist the desire for power or control.

May a spirit of service enable us to work as a team;
to see what is positive in others,
to welcome it and prize it as a gift from God.

In a spirit of service, may we go beyond our own interests,
to submit ourselves to the priorities of the group and of the parish.

May a spirit of service allow us to acknowledge gratefully
all that we receive from our ministry,
without our own needs becoming the centre of what we do.

Glory be ...

Morning

In the morning, while it was still very dark,
he got up and went out to a deserted place and there he prayed.
(Mark 1:35)

May there be peace in the beginning of each day.
May there be acknowledgement and awe
and reverencing of God.

O Lord, in the morning you hear my voice;
in the morning I plead my case to you and watch.
(Psalm 5:3)

May there be confidence in the beginning of each day.
May we open our hearts to the Lord
and rely on the Lord's response.

And very early on the first day of the week,
when the sun had risen, they went to the tomb.
When they looked up, they saw that the stone,
which was very large, had already been rolled back.
As they entered the tomb, they saw a young man … he said to them,
'Do not be alarmed; you are looking for Jesus of Nazareth,
who was crucified. He has been raised; he is not here.'
(Mark 16:2, 4-6)

May there be surprise in the beginning of each day.
May daylight bring with it the promise of newness
from the God who always goes ahead of us.

But I will sing of your might;
I will sing aloud of your steadfast love in the morning.
For you have been a fortress for me
and a refuge in the day of my distress.
(Psalm 59:16)

May there be strength in the beginning of each day.
May God's power fortify us
and make us eager for wholehearted service.

You know what time it is,
how it is now the moment for you to wake from sleep.
For salvation is nearer to us now than when we became believers;
the night is far gone, the day is near.
(Romans 13:11-12)

May there be hope in the beginning of each day.
In courage may we let go of what holds us back
and embrace God's call to be.

Let me hear of your steadfast love in the morning
for in you I put my trust.
Teach me the way I should go, for to you I lift up my soul.
(Psalm 143:8)

May there be light in the beginning of each day.
In the silence of our prayer may we listen
and feel God's hand taking us on the right path.

Prayer
Blessed be Jesus, risen from the dead, hope of each new day.
We ask you to breathe your Spirit of morning hope,
on all who have had a restless, troubled night,
on all who fight despair and make themselves get up,
on all who have slept well and wake up refreshed,
on all who look to the day ahead with apprehension.
Jesus, morning star, be in each heart today,
strengthening, comforting, challenging, inspiring.
Jesus, morning star, may we enjoy your risen life today. Amen.

You are ...

Reflection
In reality it is only in the mystery of the Word made flesh
that the mystery of who we are truly becomes clear.
The church is entrusted with the task
of opening up to humanity the mystery of God;
in doing so, it opens up to us the meaning of our own existence,
the innermost truth about ourselves.
(Vatican II)

In Jesus we find reflected the face of God,
but also our own face.
For Jesus tells us who we are
and when we gaze upon him
he reflects back to us the wonder and mystery
of our own being.

*Go around the group, each person saying one of these phrases, where Jesus,
or one of his apostles, tells us who we are:*

You are God's people

You are the salt of the earth

You are the Body of Christ

You are my friends

You are God's temple

You are led by the Spirit

You are a chosen race, a royal priesthood,
a holy nation, God's own people

You are the light of the world

You are members of the household of God

You are one in Christ Jesus

You are no longer a slave but a child
and if a child, then also an heir

You are in the Spirit

You are the branches

You are one body

If other 'you are...' phrases from scripture occur to anybody,
leave a few moments for saying them ...

Then stay in quiet for a few moments,
each person dwelling on the phrase of their choice.

Prayer
When you, O Lord, tell us who we are
we are reassured about ourselves.

When you, O Lord, tell us who we are
we feel called to become what you see.

When we, O Lord, become what you see
others see you
and are reassured about themselves.

That this may be so, we pray
through Christ our Lord. Amen.

Witness

'Woe to me if I do not proclaim the gospel!'
(Saint Paul, 1 Corinthians 9:16)

Reflection
Above all the gospel must be proclaimed by witness.

Take a Christian or a handful of Christians who,
in the midst of their own community,
show their capacity for understanding and acceptance,
their sharing of life and destiny with other people,
their solidarity with the efforts of all
for whatever is noble and good.

Let us suppose that, in addition, they radiate
in an altogether simple and unaffected way
their faith in values that go beyond current values
and their hope in something that is not seen
and that one would not dare to imagine.

Through this wordless witness these Christians
stir up irresistible questions in the hearts
of those who see how they live;
Why are they like this?
Why do they live in this way?
What or who is it that inspires them?
Why are they in our midst?
Such a witness is already a silent proclamation of the Good News
and a very powerful and effective one.

The above questions will perhaps be the first
that many non-Christians will ask,
whether they are people to whom Christ has never been proclaimed,

or baptised people who do not practise,
or people who live as nominal Christians
but according to principles that are in no way Christian,
or people who are seeking, and not without suffering,
something or someone whom they sense but cannot name.

Other questions will arise, deeper and more demanding ones,
questions evoked by this witness,
a witness which involves presence, sharing, solidarity,
and which is an essential element, and generally the first one,
in evangelisation.

All Christians are called to this witness
and in this way they can be real evangelisers.
(Pope Paul VI)

Discussion
Share with each other what each finds striking in the passage.
In what ways does it reflect the way our parish is?
In what ways does it challenge our parish?

Prayer
May we be filled with a sense of Good News
and with a desire to share Good News.
May our faith always look outward
and may it take the form of witness.
May the lives of Christians be a leaven
for the transformation of the world
and the hope of humanity. Amen.

Does God Listen?

Reflection
Are we like the old woodcutter who got a bit drunk
and lost his way home in the forest and he lay down and fell
and found himself taken before God for judgement.
And the angels wouldn't talk to him and God was cross with him –
said he drank too much and went home too late and cheated his customers
and he'd have to carry a block of wood on his back for punishment.

And the woodcutter suddenly said: 'No, I won't.
I haven't done half the things to you that you did to me.
You left me without a father and my mother died young.
I have to cheat because I am so poor and I'd starve if I did not.
My wife abuses me and the ribs on my horse stick out like fence posts.
I'll carry no block of wood for you.'

And the story says the angels stood in horror at this cheek to God.
And God? God started crying and said,
'I never knew it was like that, I am sorry. How can I make it up to you?
You can stay here and everything will be all right,
or if you prefer you can go back and give it another go.'
And the woodcutter said he would go back and try this life again.
And God said, 'Good man yourself.'

So he woke up in the forest, feeling all right and happy with himself
and he got to his hut and went in.
And immediately his wife rushed at him and hit him with the pan
and abused him for a drunken sod that was never home in time
and all the woodcutter did was look up to heaven and shake his head.
He had gone home with hope and here he was as bad as ever.
Almost, not quite.
For at least now he felt somebody saw and noticed and understood.
(Thomas Waldron)

Scripture: Does God listen?
When they cry out to me I will surely hear their cry.
(Exodus 22:23)

I love the Lord because he has heard my voice and my supplications,
because he inclined his ear to me.
(Psalm 116:1-2)

From the city the dying groan,
and the throat of the wounded cries for help;
yet God pays no attention to their prayer.
(Job 24:12)

O Lord, how long shall I cry for help and you will not listen?
(Habakkuk 1:2)

Meditation / Sharing
What has been my own experience?

Prayer
For the times we have felt the Lord inclining his ear to us,
we give thanks.
For the times we have felt the silence of God,
we give thanks.
For the times we have felt that God did not hear,
we give thanks.

We praise and thank you, our listening God
who, in your infinite silence,
hear far more than we can ever understand.

Glory be …

Meditation: Embodied Me

Scripture
Are not five sparrows sold for two pennies?
Yet not one of them is forgotten in God's sight.
But even the hairs of your head are all counted.
Do not be afraid; you are of more value than many sparrows.
(Luke 12:6-7)

Meditation
Relaxing, getting in touch with embodied me …
the story of me, my body today …

Starting with my feet,
what kind of day has it been for my feet …
what did they wear …
did they travel far, or climb or struggle …
did they have a chance to relax …
are they troubled, sweaty, blistered, sore or ignored …
I bestow a blessing on them now …

And my hands, so busy I couldn't count all they do …
what work did they do this day, washing, fixing, writing, driving …
the other bodies they touched today, blessed today …
shapes and textures they felt …
how they prayed today …
I ask them to relax as each blesses the other with a massage …

I listen to the story of my mouth …
all the tastes that my mouth has known today …
toothpaste, meals, water during the day, tea or coffee …
bad tastes I got today …
and apart from taste, did my mouth sing today, or cry …
what did my mouth say today, important words …

As I move through my body, I come to my nose …
how has my nose been today, clear or clogged …
what did I smell today …
what lovely odours – food, coffee, flowers, perfumes …
what distasteful smells, or smells of danger …
I bless my mouth and my nose for all their work today

I listen to the story of my ears today,
they have heard so much …
the morning alarm, the radio, voices, traffic,
shouting, singing, arguing …
silence perhaps …
what did I hear today that awakened me, the hope I heard …
bad news my ears received today, words of worry and concern …
the voices I heard today, the people, the stories in those voices …
I bless my ears, without which I would be so lonely …

And finally, my eyes, they register so much more
than I have time to attend to …
and into that register, that memory of my eyes I now enter …
what did my eyes see today, in the house when I got up …
in the world outside …
in the faces I encountered through the day …
all that I saw but did not notice …
I bless my eyes, for all they see and all they remember for me

And as this prayer has risen up through my body, it continues now
as I stretch out my arms and my body towards the heavens
in praise of the one who created me …

Glory be …

All Ministries are Equal

Reflection
Think about the different ministries that people are involved in.
Some ministries can appear more important than others,
perhaps because of what they achieve or because of their status
or because the activity is so attractive.
Other ministries are behind the scenes, or more of a chore.
Some of the people involved feel that their work is more important.
Others feel that what they do is not as important.

Looking beyond this, think about the people in our parish –
older and younger; richer and poorer; happy and sad;
in the mainstream and on the fringes.
Some people can appear to be more important.
Some people feel more important.
Some can appear to be less important.
Some can feel less important.

Scripture
In the Christian community in Corinth,
Paul found himself confronted with some of these problems

The body does not consist of one member but of many.
If the foot would say, 'Because I am not a hand,
I do not belong to the body,'
that would not make it any less a part of the body.
And if the ear would say, 'Because I am not an eye,
I do not belong to the body,'
that would not make it any less a part of the body.
If the whole body were an eye, where would the hearing be?
If the whole body were hearing, where would the sense of smell be?
But as it is, God arranged the members in the body,
each one of them, as he chose.

If all were a single member, where would the body be?
As it is, there are many members, yet one body.
(1 Corinthians 12:14-20)

Prayer
Response: Inspire us with your Spirit O Lord

We are committed to building up in our parish
a spirit of welcome and belonging.
May this commitment bear fruit in people having a sense
of their dignity and equality as members of the body of Christ.
May all feel that the Spirit has gifted them in a unique way.

We are committed to a spirit of humble service
in the different activities of our parish.
May this spirit pervade the work of all who minister here.
May none exaggerate their importance.
May none minimise their importance.
May all feel appreciated for the value of what they contribute.

May our sense of oneness in Christ Jesus
inspire in us feelings of harmony and solidarity
and control our temptation to compare and feel superior.
May it teach us to be thankful for one another.

Glory be...

Our Vocation to Love

Scripture
Let each of you lead the life
that the Lord has assigned,
to which God called you.
(1 Corinthians 7:17)

Prayers
We pray for all God's people
in the different ways and the different circumstances
in which they live their lives and their calling.

Response: Praised be God for our vocation to love.

Religious Life
Compassionate God, bless those of us
who live out the call to love in religious life.
We pray for them; may they be a sign to the church,
challenging it to a less complacent, more urgent following of Jesus.

Married
Compassionate God, bless those of us
who live out the call to love in marriage.
Through their appreciation of one another,
may they see their different personalities flower.
We pray for them, that their relationship may proclaim
to the church and to the world
the respect and cherishing due to each person

Widowed
Compassionate God, bless those of us
who live out the call to love as widowed people.
We pray for their peace and protection;

we pray that they will be free to go on inviting forth
the love that is in others around them.

Ordained
Compassionate God, bless those of us
who live out the call to love as priests.
We pray for them as they lead us in prayer.
May they reveal to your people the call to love
that is the core of our being

Single
Compassionate God, bless those of us
who live out the call to love as single people.
We pray for their happiness and that they will go on being a gift
to all whom they come in contact with.

Renewal of Love
We bless you, Lord, and we praise you,
for your love is everlasting.
We thank you for the love we have experienced in life.
We bless you for the opportunities we have had
to enrich the lives of others.
We acknowledge the love that has sustained us
in sad and difficult times.
Teach us to love well
and to overcome the obstacles in our own hearts.
May our love be for others the aroma
of your boundless and inclusive love.
May it increase the peace in the world.
Amen.

Prayer for the Year Ahead

As we gather together to begin a new year's work
we turn to the God of newness, the God of creation and imagination,
the God who has created everything new in the resurrection of Jesus,
the God whose Spirit renews our souls and renews the face of the earth.

When you send forth your Spirit they are created;
and you renew the face of the earth.
(Psalm 104:30)

Do not remember the former things,
or consider the things of old.
I am about to do a new thing;
now it springs forth,
do you not perceive it?
(Isaiah 43:18-19)

And the one who was seated on the throne said,
'See, I am making all things new.'
(Revelation 21:5)

As we plan our year's work,
we may think we know what lies before us in the year ahead,
but we do not know what new things the Lord will bring about before our eyes.
We open ourselves in hope-filled expectation to the God of surprises,
as we ask ourselves:

What am I looking forward to in the group's work this year?
Is there anything I am less enthusiastic about?
What do I hope we achieve in the year ahead?

Quiet / Sharing

Prayers
Response: Renew us with your Spirit, O Lord

For ourselves as a group
May we listen well when another speaks;
may we appreciate each other's views and gifts;
may we be open to learning;
may we enjoy working as a team.

For our parish
May more and more people find in this parish
an experience of welcome and of home.
Through the ministry of our parish
may many people come to know the God of love.

For each of ourselves
Spirit of the risen Lord,
rouse us with excitement at the signs of hope around us;
fire us with enthusiasm for our calling,
to serve God's plan in our time and place;
ignite us with energy and passion for our task.

For the work that lies ahead
Bless us Lord with the practicality of Martha
and with the reflective spirit of Mary
as we sit at your feet in prayer,
as we go about doing your work.

Glory be …

Spring Rain

The Lord will come to us like the spring rain
with blessings and growth and new life

Do not fear, O Jacob my servant, whom I have chosen.
For I will pour water on the thirsty land
and streams on the dry ground;
I will pour my spirit upon your descendants
and my blessings on your offspring.
They shall spring up like a green tamarisk,
like willows by flowing streams.
This one will say, 'I am the Lord's',
another will be called by the name of Jacob.
(Isaiah 44:2-5)

Lord, calm our fear
and build up our confidence.
May our hope be assured
that your life will spring forth
and more hearts will proclaim your name.

After two days he will revive us;
on the third day he will raise us up,
that we may live before him.
Let us know, let us press on to know the Lord;
his appearing is as sure as the dawn;
he will come to us like the showers,
like the spring rains that water the earth.
(Hosea 6:2-3)

In these days of dying and new birth in our church,
let us let go of what is past and press on to what lies ahead
on the path the Lord opens before us.

Be patient, therefore, beloved,
until the coming of the Lord.
The farmer waits for the precious crop from the earth,
being patient with it until it receives
the early and the late rains.
You also must be patient.
Strengthen your hearts
for the coming of the Lord is near.
(James 5:7-8)

May your pace be our pace, O Lord,
may our hearts beat with yours;
may your time be our time.

I will make them and the region around my hill a blessing;
and I will send down the showers in their season;
they shall be showers of blessing.
The trees of the field shall yield their fruit
and the earth shall yield its increase.
(Ezekiel 34:26-27)

We praise you Lord,
constant source of life,
surprising source of blessing,
irrepressible source of hope.

Conclusion
Blessed be the Lord
whose power is at work amongst us
whose word and promise refresh us like spring rain.
May God's kingdom come!

Glory be ...

Remembering our Confirmation

Scripture
The disciples rejoiced when they saw the Lord.
Jesus said to them again, 'Peace be with you.
As the Father has sent me, so I send you.'
When he had said this, he breathed on them
and said to them, 'Receive the Holy Spirit.'
(John 20:20-22)

Reflection
Confirmation does highlight a special aspect
of membership of the church. In this sacrament,
more clearly and more explicitly than in baptism,
a person is commissioned
to take on *responsibility for the church's task*
and to become actively involved in pursuing it.

The solemnity of this commissioning
is brought out by the *rites*. There is first of all
the very ancient gesture, 'the imposition of hands'.
It is an invocation of the Holy Spirit to assist people in
fulfilling *public* tasks to which they are being commissioned.

Another pointer to the meaning of confirmation
is the use of the ancient rite of anointing with oil.
This has to do with 'christening'.
It means that a person becomes a Christ-figure in the world.
It is a *Christ-ening*.
As a sign that we have taken on the Anointed One's name
and the Anointed One's task in the world,
we are anointed in confirmation – as we are in baptism –
with the holy oil of Chrism.
(Enda Lyons)

Prayers
Response: Confirm us, Lord, in your love

Through this sacrament,
the grace of baptism has been confirmed in us.
May we walk with confidence,
assured of our dignity as sons and daughters of God.

Through this sacrament, we are given a mission,
to confirm others in a sense of God's love
and of divine providence in their lives.
May we grow into this mission.

May more baptised, confirmed Christians become aware
of their responsibility and calling
to build Christian community and to heal the world.

Blessing Prayer
Together we say, to each baptised, confirmed person in our parish,
including ourselves, a prayer of blessing and hope:

You are a treasured person in this parish family.
You are a gift of God to us.
Always know that you are welcome here.
Now that you are confirmed in the Holy Spirit,
we pray that God's Spirit will be alive in you,
bearing fruit in love and joy,
peace and patience,
kindness, generosity and faithfulness,
gentleness and self-control.

Glory be …

Our Names

'Rejoice that your names are written in heaven.' (Luke 10:20)

Sharing
Begin with a few moments silence to allow people to gather their thoughts.

Invite each person in turn to say something about his or her name.
What name appears on your birth certificate? Why was it chosen?
Has your name been changed or shortened over the years? Nicknames?
How do you feel about your name?
What do you prefer to be called?

Meditation
Invite the participants to get into a relaxed position and to quieten themselves.

Think of our respect for God's name …
'Thou shalt not take the name of thy God in vain.'
'Hallowed be thy name.'
'His name will be called Jesus.'

Each of our names is precious, representing our story and our dignity …
'God calls each one by name. Everyone's name is sacred.
The name is the icon of the person.
It demands respect as a sign of the dignity of the one who bears it.'
(Catechism, 2158)

This respect can be lacking …
'Excuse me, but I forget your name.'
'Which John/Mary are you?'
Being called names.
Having your name misspelled or mispronounced.

Think of those who treasure you and your name.
Imagine them saying your name,
how it sounds when said by each of these people.
Think of the different sides of you
that each of these persons brings out.

Think now of God naming us. Think of naming in the bible,
how God's naming says something about the one named.
We too are named by God, our name is a symbol
of God's faithfulness to us …

'Do not fear for I have redeemed you.
I have called you by name, you are mine.'
(Isaiah 43:1)
'Can a woman forget her nursing child
or show no compassion for the child of her womb?
Even these may forget, yet I will not forget you.
See, I have inscribed you on the palms of my hands.'
(Isaiah 49:15-16)
'I will give them an everlasting name that shall not be cut off.'
(Isaiah 56:5)
'You shall be called by a new name that the mouth of the Lord will give.
You shall be a crown of beauty in the hand of the Lord.'
(Isaiah 62:2-3)

Think of Jesus calling people by name:
'Levi' … 'Mary' … 'Simon' … 'Martha' … 'Lazarus'.

Think of how he cherishes each of these persons.
Imagine Jesus calling you by name.
Imagine Jesus bestowing beauty on you in saying your name –
affirming your dignity, calling you from your prison,
calling you to discipleship.

Think of a word (e.g. 'strength', 'harmony') and/or
a symbol (e.g. flower, rainbow) to go with your name.

Prayer
We rejoice that our names are written in heaven
and we praise the Lord
who has called us into being,
who loves us with an everlasting love,
who delights in our very being.

Glory be…

Welcome

God's heart is a welcoming heart, reaching out in Jesus to embrace all.
We listen to the theme of welcome in the gospels – its presence and its absence.

People welcome Jesus
Mary said, 'Here am I, the servant of the Lord;
let it be with me according to your word.'
(Luke 1:38)

Now as they went on their way, he entered a certain village
where a woman named Martha welcomed him into her home.
She had a sister named Mary who sat at the Lord's feet
and listened to what he was saying.
(Luke10:38)

Others do not welcome Jesus
Herod said to the wise men, 'Go and search diligently for the child;
and when you have found him, bring me word,
so that I may also go and pay him homage.'
(Matthew 2:8)

He was in the world, yet the world did not know him.
He came to what was his own
and his own people did not accept him.
(John 1:11-12)

Jesus welcomes us
'Come to me, all you that are weary
and are carrying heavy burdens and I will give you rest.
Take my yoke upon you and learn from me for I am gentle
and humble in heart, and you will find rest for your souls.
For my yoke is easy and my burden is light.'
(Matthew 11:28-30)

And the Pharisees and the scribes were grumbling and saying,
'This fellow welcomes sinners and eats with them.'
(Luke 15:2)

Jesus said to them, 'Let the little children come to me;
do not stop them; for it is to such as these
that the kingdom of God belongs.'
(Mark 10:14)

Jesus tells us of God's welcoming heart
'But while he [the prodigal son]was still far off,
his father saw him and was filled with compassion;
he ran and put his arms around him and kissed him.'
(Luke 15:20)

We are called to welcome
Welcome one another just as Christ has welcomed you
for the glory of God.
(Romans 15:7)

'Whoever welcomes you welcomes me and whoever
welcomes me welcomes the one who sent me.'
(Matthew 10:40)

We fail to welcome
There was a rich man who was dressed in purple and fine linen
and who feasted sumptuously every day.
And at his gate lay a poor man named Lazarus,
covered with sores, who longed to satisfy his hunger
with what fell from the rich man's table.
(Luke 16:19-21)

Prayer
May our hearts be filled with the welcome that fills God's heart.
May we know God's welcome for ourselves.
May we appreciate God's welcome for all God's people.
May we cultivate a welcoming heart
and communicate God's welcome in our world.

Glory be …

The Trinity Within

(1)
God lives in us, Father, Son and Spirit,
in the gifts of faith, hope and love.

Reflection
Listen to the Word – you are God's beloved.
God lives within you,
closer to you than your very self,
your assurance that all is well.
This is the gift of faith.

Listen to the Word – you are the Body of Christ.
Christ's life flows through you
and flows through us all,
linking us together.
This is the gift of love.

Listen to the Word – you are the temple of the Spirit.
Divine energy and inspiration fills you,
your resource in all life's troubles,
your perseverance and enthusiasm.
This is the gift of hope.

Prayer
Holy Trinity, Father, Son and Holy Spirit
living within us
in the gifts of faith, hope and love;
may you grow in us
and may we grow into you.

(2)
God lives in us, Father, Son and Spirit,
when we activate our gifts in service.

Scripture
Now there are varieties of gifts,
but the same Spirit;
and there are varieties of services,
but the same Lord;
and there are varieties of activities,
but it is the same God
who activates all of them in everyone.
To each is given
the manifestation of the Spirit
for the common good.
(1 Corinthians 12:4-7)

Prayer
Spirit of new life,
make us confident of our gifts
and appreciative of the gifts of others.

Lord of our salvation,
inspire us in a spirit of service
dedicated to building up your Body.

God our creator,
release love's energy in our hearts
and make it real and active in our lives.

As you become active in us
may we become part of you.

Glory be ...

Our Parish

Scripture
I am the vine, you are the branches.
Those who abide in me and I in them bear much fruit
because apart from me you can do nothing.
(John 15:5)

Reflection
I want you to imagine in front of you a most wonderful tree.
This tree represents our parish. From its trunk we can tell its age.
Over the years it has weathered many a storm, including recent times.
Many branches are strong and sturdy, some are worse for wear.
Others are young and are braving the elements.

Each branch represents an area of our parish and of our belief system.
Take a moment to become aware of this tree
and the many different areas in our parish that it symbolises.
Many branches are obvious. Others are tucked away from sight,
but all contribute to the overall grandeur of the tree.
You may wish to stand back from it and admire it
or you may wish to sit under it with your back to the trunk
and feel the massive support therein.

You may find as you look at this tree, its branches, its leaves,
that some of the leaves have withered and turned brown.
There are signs that from time to time branches have fallen off.
Over time many branches have grown old and decayed
and have fallen to the base of the tree. Others have been cut off.
These leaves and branches, though decayed and rotten,
have replenished the earth and nourished the roots of the tree.

Become aware of the strength that comes with having secure roots
that are constantly being nourished. Nothing is ever lost.
Every idea our parish has had, whether used or discarded,
has led to where we are today and to who we are today.
Many ideas have blown in on the wind.

Some have remained.
Others have been blown around elsewhere, only to be
replenished and recycled and to come back stronger than ever.

Each branch represents some aspect of parish life.
Some are very strong and support smaller branches and leaves.
But all the branches are needed to give this parish its identity
and to support and comfort all who come within its compass.
This tree has room for us all. All of our ideas and needs
will hopefully find support and nourishment here.

The firm trunk represents our faith, which is deeply rooted
in our belief in Jesus Christ and in the scriptures –
the Good News which gives us our depth,
and the nourishment and support that we need.
Each new branch and leaf that appears shows our learning,
our growth and our faith development.

Over the years the shape of the tree has changed.
It will need to continue to change,
to suit the environment and the needs of the day.
It will need to be pruned and fed, so that it continues to provide
the best nourishment and support for those who depend on it.

Similarly, as a parish we too will need to change.
We need to be open to new ideas and viewpoints that are
different from our own, in order to keep alive and productive
the great gift of faith and community that we have here in our parish.
(Anne Daly)

Prayer
For all that has been in our parish, we say 'thanks',
for those who have gone ahead of us,
for their faith and their care, and the spirit they have left with us.

For all that will be in our parish, we say 'yes',
for the possibilities that will present themselves,
for the potential that will reveal itself.

Glory be …

Matthew, Evangelist

This prayer is composed around texts that appear only in Matthew's gospel.

ESCAPE TO EGYPT

An angel of the Lord appeared to Joseph in a dream and said,
'Get up, take the child and his mother and flee to Egypt,
and remain there until I tell you;
for Herod is about to search for the child, to destroy him.'
Then Joseph got up, took the child and his mother by night
and went to Egypt, and remained there until the death of Herod.
(Matthew 2:13-15)

Prayer
We pray for parents who live in fear.
We pray for fathers, for the gift of responsible caring.
We pray for families dispossessed, or forced to flee or emigrate.

TWO SONS

'What do you think? A man had two sons; he went to the first
and said, 'Son, go and work in the vineyard today.'
He answered, 'I will not'; but later he changed his mind and went.
The father went to the second and said the same; and he answered,
'I go, sir'; but he did not go. Which of the two did the will of his father?'
They said, 'The first.' Jesus said to them,
'Truly I tell you, the tax collectors and the prostitutes
are going into the kingdom of God ahead of you.'
(Matthew 21:28-31)

Prayer
For the gift of being able to change our mind and admit we are wrong;
for the gift of repentance and the conquest of our self-righteousness;
for a humble, non-judgemental attitude and the gift of compassion;
we pray to you, O Lord.

COMMUNITY
'Truly I tell you, if two of you agree on earth
about anything you ask, it will be done for you
by my Father in heaven.
For where two or three are gathered in my name
I am there among them.'
(Matthew 18:19-20)

Prayer
May we experience the grace of togetherness.
May we feel Christ present in our love and in our conversation,
in our prayer together and in our partnership.

TREASURE
'The kingdom of heaven is like treasure hidden in a field,
which someone found and hid; then in his joy he goes
and sells all that he has and buys that field. Again,
the kingdom of heaven is like a merchant in search of fine pearls;
on finding one pearl of great value, he went
and sold all that he had and bought it.'
(Matthew 13:44-45)

Prayer
We hope that faith will be as exciting as this for each of us.
We hope that we will be willing to pay the price
to make our dreams come true.
We hope that all who are searching will discover,
and be surprised with joy.

Concluding Prayer
We praise you, our God, for the unique ways
in which Matthew unveils for us the mystery of Jesus Christ.
May the word of the gospel sink deep in our hearts.
May the ripples radiate out into our lives and into the world.

Mark, Evangelist

This prayer is composed around texts that appear only in Mark's gospel.

GROWING SEED

'The kingdom of God is as if
someone would scatter seed on the ground
and would sleep and rise, night and day,
and the seed would sprout and grow, he does not know how.
The earth produces of itself, first the stalk, then the head,
then the full grain in the head.
But when the grain is ripe, at once he goes in with his sickle,
because the harvest has come.'
(Mark 4:26-29)

Prayer
May we have a deep sense of amazement at the ways
in which your kingdom, O Lord, springs forth in the world.
Give us eyes to see the signs of hope in our midst.

A BLIND MAN

They came to Bethsaida.
Some people brought a blind man to him
and begged him to touch him.
He took the blind man by the hand and led him out of the village;
and when he had put saliva on his eyes
and laid his hands on him, he asked him,
'Can you see anything?' And the man looked up and said,
'I can see people, but they look like trees, walking.'
Then Jesus laid his hands on his eyes again;
and he looked intently and his sight was restored
and he saw everything clearly.
(Mark 8:22-25)

Prayer
Lord, bless those who gently bring us, in our blindness, to you.
Allow us to experience the disciple's gradual journey of enlightenment.
Save us from complacency, make us always eager to see more.

RELEASE
They brought to him a deaf man who had an impediment in his speech
and they begged him to lay his hand on him.
He took him aside in private, away from the crowd
and put his fingers into his ears and he spat and touched his tongue.
Then looking up to heaven he sighed and said to him,
'Ephphatha,' that is, 'Be opened.'
And immediately his ears were opened,
his tongue was released and he spoke plainly.
(Mark 7:32-35)

Prayer
For people who have difficulty speaking;
For people who have difficulty hearing;
For the gift of listening to and hearing what God says;
For the energy to proclaim Good News with our lives;
we pray to you, O Lord.

Concluding Prayer
We praise you, our God, for the unique ways
in which Mark unveils for us the mystery of Jesus Christ.
May the word of the gospel sink deep in our hearts.
May the ripples radiate out into our lives and into the world.

Glory be …

Luke, Evangelist

This prayer is composed around texts that appear only in Luke's gospel.

EXPECT NOTHING

'If you lend to those from whom you hope to receive,
what credit is that to you?
Even sinners lend to sinners, to receive as much again.
But love your enemies, do good and lend,
expecting nothing in return.'

He also said to one who had invited him,
'When you give a luncheon or a dinner, do not invite
your friends or your brothers or your relatives or rich neighbours,
in case they may invite you in return and you would be repaid.
But when you give a banquet,
invite the poor, the crippled, the lame and the blind.
And you will be blessed, because they cannot repay you.'
(Luke 6:34-35; 14:12-14)

Prayer
Let this gospel spirit of giving without expectation of return
penetrate the hearts and attitudes of many.
May this spirit of other-centred concern
challenge our self-regarding world.

BUILDING A TOWER

'Whoever does not carry the cross and follow me cannot be my disciple.
For which of you, intending to build a tower, does not first sit down
and estimate the cost, to see whether he has enough to complete it?
Otherwise, when he has laid a foundation and is not able to finish,
all who see it will begin to ridicule him, saying,
'This fellow began to build and was not able to finish.'
(Luke 14:27-30)

Prayer
Lord, let us not grow casual about discipleship and its demands.
Let us be open-eyed about what you ask of us.
Let us be single-minded in our response.

PRAYER
Jesus told them a parable about their need
to pray always and not to lose heart. He said,
'In a certain city there was a judge who neither feared God
nor had respect for people. In that city
there was a widow who kept coming to him and saying,
'Grant me justice against my opponent.'
For a while he refused, but later he said to himself,
'Though I have no fear of God and no respect for anyone,
yet because this widow keeps bothering me, I will grant her justice,
so that she may not wear me out by continually coming.'
And the Lord said, 'Listen to what the unjust judge says.
And will not God grant justice to his chosen ones
who cry to him day and night?
Will he delay long in helping them?'
(Luke 18:1-7)

Prayer
May we not lose heart, our every thought an act of trust in God.
May all who cry out be granted the experience of God's justice.

Concluding Prayer
We praise you, our God, for the unique ways
in which Luke unveils for us the mystery of Jesus Christ.
May the word of the gospel sink deep in our hearts.
May the ripples radiate out into our lives and into the world.

Glory be ...

John, Evangelist

This prayer is composed around texts that appear only in John's gospel.

THE WORD

In the beginning was the Word and the Word was with God
and the Word was God. He was in the beginning with God.
All things came into being through him and without him
not one thing came into being. What has come into being in him
was life, and the life was the light of all people.
The light shines in the darkness and the darkness did not overcome it …
And the Word became flesh and lived among us,
and we have seen his glory.' *(John 1:1-5,14)*

Prayer
Lord, shine light in our darkness.
May your Word become flesh today.
May our words reflect what your Word expresses.

JESUS AND THOMAS

Jesus came and stood among them and said,
'Peace be with you.'
Then he said to Thomas,
'Put your finger here and see my hands.
Reach out your hand and put it in my side.
Do not doubt, but believe.'
Thomas answered him, 'My Lord and my God!'
Jesus said to him,
'Have you believed because you have seen me?
Blessed are those who have not seen
and yet have come to believe.' *(John 20:26-29)*

Prayer
May we trust in the eyes of our heart, the eyes of our faith,
to see more clearly, to see more deeply,
the mystery that is life, the mystery that is God.

BETHZATHA POOL

Now in Jerusalem by the Sheep Gate there is a pool,
called in Hebrew Bethzatha, which has five porticoes.
In these lay many invalids – blind, lame and paralysed.
One man was there who had been ill for thirty-eight years.
When Jesus saw him lying there and knew that he had been there a long time,
he said to him, 'Do you want to be made well?' *(John 5:2-6)*

Prayer
We reach out to all who suffer silently, who suffer year after year.
May we notice them as Jesus did.
May they not lose touch with the wishing and wanting in their hearts.

LAZARUS

Then Jesus, again greatly distressed, came to the tomb.
It was a cave and a stone was lying against it. Jesus said,
'Take away the stone.' He cried with a loud voice, 'Lazarus, come out!'
The dead man came out, his hands and feet bound with strips of cloth,
and his face wrapped in a cloth. Jesus said to them,
'Unbind him and let him go.' *(John 11:38-39,43-44)*

Prayer
May we hear your voice, Lord, shouting into our darkness,
where life is blocked up within us.
Free us from what binds and imprisons us.
Inspire us to bring out the best in each other.

Concluding Prayer
We praise you, our God, for the unique ways
in which John unveils for us the mystery of Jesus Christ.
May the word of the gospel sink deep in our hearts.
May the ripples radiate out into our lives and into the world.

Glory be ...

Our Commitments

Scripture
'See, I have set before you today life and prosperity,
death and adversity. If you obey the commandments
of the Lord your God that I am commanding you today
by loving the Lord your God, walking in his ways
and observing his commandments, decrees and ordinances,
then you shall live and become numerous, and the Lord your God
will bless you in the land that you are entering to possess.
Choose life so that you and your descendants may live,
loving the Lord your God, obeying him and holding fast to him;
for that means life to you and length of days.'
(Deuteronomy 30:15-16, 19-20)

Reflection
Each of us makes our life decisions;
each of us chooses a path to follow,
a value to live by,
another to love.
Each of us chooses and is chosen,
each of us both takes a path and is shown a path.
For some of us, the choice lies ahead,
for others it is long since made;
others again are wrestling with deciding,
others are reviewing and choosing again.
In quiet prayer, we place our commitments before you, Lord,
you who have committed yourself completely to us.

Prayer
We pray to the God of promise and expectation
to bless our commitments, whatever point they are at,
whether we are assured or struggling,
surviving or rejoicing
or still exploring.

God our creator,
in Jesus Christ you have bound yourself to humanity
in a bond that cannot be broken.
From earliest times, your people called you
'rock' and 'stronghold' and 'mighty fortress',
as they came to appreciate
your absolute loyalty and utter dependability.
In Jesus' heart of love you have given the world
the enduring statement, that you are everlasting, faithful love.

In all the power of who you are,
bless each one here on the journey of commitment.
Bless each one with the gifts
that will enhance their joy on the journey –
the gift of listening,
the gift of putting others first,
the gift of self-knowledge,
the gift of reliability and faithfulness,
the gift of energy,
the gift of reflection.

As you bless us, may each of us experience,
in our hearts and in our lives, even a shadow or a hint
of the unspeakable, incomparable mystery of love that you are.

As you bless us, we bless you
for all that you mean to us, through Jesus Christ our Lord.

Reconciliation – Church

Reflection
We pray for the Spirit, for the divine power of reconciliation,
the Spirit that makes all things new.

We bring before God
needs that loom very large in our lives –
the need to be able to forgive
and the need to believe that we are forgiven;
the need to let go of resentment
and the need to accept the possibility of new beginnings.

We experience these needs in so many ways ...
In times of taking for granted and times of being taken for granted;
of being intolerant and of not being tolerated;
In times of deceiving and times of being deceived;
of not listening and of not being listened to;
In times of being cruel and times of being treated unkindly;
of not seeing from the other's side and of not being understood;
of not communicating and of not being communicated to;
In times of being judgemental and times of being judged.

We feel these needs, not just as human beings, but also as Christians,
as members of a church that proclaims a gospel of forgiveness –
such a powerful gospel, inspired by the vision and lifestyle of Jesus –
yet a gospel that is carried in such weak hands.
Sorrowfully we acknowledge that our church is a place
where courtesy and gentleness can be lacking,
where trust can be missing,
where respect can be absent for people in different situations,
where sympathy for the circumstances of people's lives can be wanting.

Bearing these needs, we pray for the Spirit of reconciliation
to breathe into our families and relationships and all the hurts therein
and into the pain of our larger family, our church.

Scripture
If anyone is in Christ there is a new creation;
everything old has passed away; see, everything has become new!
All this is from God, who reconciled himself to us in Christ
and has given us the ministry of reconciliation.
(2 Corinthians 5:17-18)

Prayers
Response: O God of peace, make your people new.

We pray for the church. May it be humble and hospitable,
gracious and generous, repentant and renewed.

In our prayer we reach out to homes and relationships
where love is blocked by the inability to forgive and be forgiven.
We pray for God's healing of all this accumulated pain.

We pray for the qualities that allow us to accept forgiveness –
believing that we can start again; confessing when we are wrong;
not needing to be always in the right.

We pray for the qualities that allow us to forgive –
letting go of resentment; stepping into the other's shoes;
understanding that it could have been me.

Spirit of Jesus Christ, through the power of the resurrection,
we are a new creation, entrusted with the ministry of reconciliation.
May we live as a new creation in all our relationships
and may our life as a faith community be permeated
with the Spirit of reconciliation and hope.

Glory be ...

Christians are Missionaries

Scripture
How are they to call on one
in whom they have not believed?
And how are they to believe in one
of whom they have never heard?
And how are they to hear
without someone to proclaim him?
And how are they to proclaim him
unless they are sent?
As it is written,
'how beautiful are the feet of those
who bring good news.'
(Romans 10:14-15)

Reflection
Lord, I feel inadequate and small before the awesome truth
that it is through people like me
that your gospel is proclaimed and heard;
that people like me are your voice and your heart in the world.
But, inadequate as I am,
God forbid that I should ever feel adequate or suitable or capable,
as if everything depended on me.
May I always feel empty,
ready to be filled with you rather than myself.
Work through me Lord, speak your word
through the giftedness you have blessed me with,
through the dedication and energy and humility
of my empty heart.

Prayers
Response: Praised be Jesus.

Praised be Jesus for the people through whom
I have heard the good news of the gospel ...
I pause to think of God's missionaries to me.

Praised be Jesus for the many ways in which
people communicate to each other the love of God –
missionaries without knowing it.

Praised be Jesus whose Spirit empowers me
as a missionary of God's kingdom,
whose power is at work in me.

Praised be Jesus, who calls us together;
we are united in sharing his dream,
we are bonded with his ties of friendship.
we are joined in bringing about his future.

Prayer
May life in our Christian community
be modelled on the life of the God we believe in,
Father, Son and Holy Spirit,
an infinite and endless giving and receiving of love.
May we graciously receive God's love from one another
and generously give that love in return.
We ask this through Christ our Lord. Amen.

For Older People

We are the people who have more to look back on
with most of our treasured times in the past
and for some of us, with all our treasured times now gathered.

Sometimes we are described as the people of memories
unlike others, whose youth makes them people of expectation;
we tend to look back where others look forward.

We praise you, God, for our memories;
we praise you for revealing to us the mystery of love,
for the grace of having known love in life,
for having been loved and been able to love in return.

But is it true that we have more memories than expectations,
that we look back rather than forward?
We think of our faith, which also looks back,
farther than we can remember, back two thousand years,
to Jesus who changed our lives,
to Jesus who is changing our lives
to Jesus who will change our lives.

Our faith in Christ is memory but also expectation.
Remembering your Son fills our hearts with expectation
of a future where you will be everything,
when we will discover, in total joy and exhilaration,
that love never dies.

Scripture
Listen to me, O house of Jacob, all the remnant of the house of Israel
who have been borne by me from your birth,
carried from the womb; even to your old age I am he,
even when you turn grey I will carry you.
I have made and I will bear; I will carry and will save.
(Isaiah 46:3-4)

Prayers
Response: We bless the Lord, who has shown us love.

May God's Spirit touch all amongst us who are widowed,
who have lost the woman or man we loved and lived for,
that we can bear our loss in a spirit of gratitude and expectation.

May God's Spirit touch all amongst us
who are in the autumn of our life,
that the prospect of ageing will not sadden us,
that we may cling with confidence
to the One who has always been with us.

May God's Spirit touch all amongst us who are lonely
from a loss that cannot be compensated for,
and give us a desire to live
and a confidence in God's providence.

May God's Spirit touch all amongst us who are disappointed by life,
for whom life has not always been the joy it can be,
that we can stay faithful to what we believe
which is the ultimate mystery of love.

May God's Spirit be with us as we remember our dead –
husband or wife, child or parent,
brother or sister, friend or relation.
Our communion on earth is our foretaste
of the communion of saints beyond time and beyond imagination,
where all the beloved will live love's fulness in God.

Glory be ...

The Spirit of Partnership

Reflection
A familiar sight and sound in Autumn
are the geese as they fly over us, heading for their wintering grounds
in the slobland around the coast, flying in a 'V' formation.
It is interesting to know what science has discovered about why they fly
that way…

It has been learned that, as each bird flaps its wings,
it creates an uplift for the bird immediately following.
By flying in a 'V' formation, the whole flock adds
over 70% greater flying range than if each bird flew on its own.

People who share a common direction and sense of community
can get where they are going quicker and easier
because they are travelling on the thrust of one another.

Whenever a goose falls out of formation,
it suddenly feels the drag and resistance of trying to do it alone
and quickly gets into formation,
to take advantage of the lifting power of the bird community in front.

If we have as much sense as a goose, we will stay in formation
with those who are headed the same way we are going.

When the lead goose gets tired, he or she rotates back in the wing
and another bird flies point.

It pays to take turns doing the hard tasks and sharing leadership.
As with geese, people are interdependent on each others' skills,
capabilities and unique combination of gifts, talents and resources.

The geese flying south in formation honk to encourage
those up front to keep up their speed.

We need to make sure that our honking is encouraging.
In groups where there is encouragement, the production is much greater.
The power of encouragement is the quality of honking we appreciate.

Finally, when a goose gets sick, wounded or shot down,
two geese drop out of formation and follow it down, to help and protect it.
They stay with it until it dies or is able to fly again.
Then they launch out with another formation or else catch up with the flock.

If we have as much sense as geese, we will stand by each other
in difficult times as well as when we are strong.
(Source unknown)

Prayers
Response: Lord, build us up in a spirit of partnership.

'None of us is as wise as all of us are.'
On this day, we let go of thinking only our own thoughts
and seeing things only our own way.
We commit ourselves to building up a shared outlook.
We commit ourselves to the open listening
and mutual appreciation that this demands.

'Strength lies in togetherness'
For this day, we let go of the false independence
of relying only on our own strength.
We commit ourselves to moulding ourselves into a strong team.
We commit ourselves to the learning that this demands –
learning to trust and learning to encourage each other.

'The Spirit is given to each, for the common good of all.'
During this day, we let go of presuming
that everything depends on us.
While we put our hearts into everything,
we pray that God's Spirit, who speaks through all of us,
will make us wise.
We pray that the Spirit, working in each one of us,
will make us strong.

Glory be ...

Offertory

Reflecting on the presentation of gifts at Mass, as a moment when our offering of ourselves and Jesus' giving of himself are joined together.

Scripture
I appeal to you, brothers and sisters by the mercies of God
to present your bodies as a living sacrifice
holy and acceptable to God, which is your spiritual worship.
(Romans 12:1)

He looked up and saw rich people putting their gifts into the treasury;
he also saw a poor widow put in two small copper coins.
He said to them: 'Truly I tell you, this poor widow
has put in more than all of them;
for all of them have contributed out of their abundance,
but she out of her poverty has put in all she had to live on.'
(Luke 21:1-4)

One of his disciples, Andrew, Simon Peter's brother, said to him,
'There is a boy here who has five barley loaves and two fish.
But what are they among so many people?'
(John 6:8-9)

Reflection
It is the weekend.
Time for rest and relaxation, and also time for worship, for church.
But as I approach the door of the church
I pause to reflect: what am I bringing with me?
I bring with me what I am – my family, my work, my relationships;
my efforts, my failures, my hopes and tears.

Sometimes I have to leave all this at the door of the church,
because I know that it won't be taken up.
What goes on in there and what goes on in me
are two different worlds and no connection will be made for me.

Sometimes it is I who fail to see the link.
My daily life seems an ocean apart from this ritual.
I cannot see how they might connect.
I am not even sure why I am here.

Sometimes I go in the door and I bring all this with me.
As the ritual moves from the lectern to the altar,
from Word to Eucharist,
as the gifts are brought up to the altar,
I find myself called, addressed.
I am not to watch this movement with gifts to the altar.
I am to take part.

From where I sit, I join myself to the procession.
There is bread; there is wine; there is me.
My hopes and failures, my family and friends, my work,
my heart, my nothing, my all. And not just me;
all of us, in our littleness and our greatness, are offertory.

As we join ourselves with the bread and wine,
we become part of what is to be transformed in this Eucharist.
Life and liturgy merge.

Quiet
Choose one of the gospel texts above, whichever you are drawn to, and
allow it to speak to you.

Prayer
May God's people see in their daily lives
moments of grace and revelation.
May they confidently bring to the altar
all that they are and all that they strive to be
however little it may seem.
May our Eucharist transform us
and release God's power in our lives.
Amen.

Saints and Souls

In the first week of November we celebrate All Saints and All Souls, as well as the Feast of all the Saints of Ireland. A week to rejoice in the communion of saints, and to remember those who have died.

ALL SAINTS

Scripture
You are no longer strangers and aliens
but you are citizens with the saints
and also members of the household of God
built upon the foundations of the apostles and prophets
with Christ Jesus himself as the cornerstone.
In him the whole structure is joined together
and grows into a holy temple in the Lord
in whom you also are built together spiritually
into a dwelling place for God.
(Ephesians 2:19-22)

Prayers
We recall the saints after whom we are named.
We recall those who have been inspirational figures in our own lives,
saints living and dead.

We pause before the mystery of what we are and what we cannot see –
that we are the Body of Christ, partakers in the communion of saints,
a communion that spans heaven and earth, life and after life.

The saints in heaven pray with us and for us.
We rely on their intercession as we pray quietly,
for ourselves, for each other, for the world.

Belonging to the communion of saints, we pray:
may what each one of us does and what each one of us suffers
bear fruit for the good of all.

ALL SOULS

Reflection
Even when dead, we are not at all separated from one another,
because we all run the same course
and we will find one another again in the same place.
We shall never be separated,
for we live in Christ,
and now we are united with Christ as we go towards him.
(St Symeon)

Prayers
We remember our own dead and our own sadness ...
Tears speak out our grief, but they also witness to our love
and we are glad to have loved so much that we can cry.
May those we have loved rest in your embrace, O Lord.

We remember the loss and grief of others around us.
We think of the funerals we have been at in the last year.
We pray especially for those who are without consolation.

Wherever there is grief, may hope be allowed to enter in
and sit beside it, as its silent companion.
May we learn to believe what we cannot see,
that our life is hidden with Christ in God.

Glory be ...

Justice

Justice is God's dream for God's people.
When the Israelites saw it, they said to one another,
'What is it?' For they did not know what it was.
Moses said to them, 'It is the bread that the Lord has given you to eat.
This is what the Lord has commanded:
'Gather as much of it as each of you needs,
an omer to a person according to the number of persons,
all providing for those in their own tents.'
The Israelites did so, some gathering more, some less.
But when they measured it with an omer,
those who gathered much had nothing over
and those who gathered little had no shortage;
they gathered as much as each of them needed.
(Exodus 16:15-18)

We pray
Praised be God our creator for dreaming this dream for us,
of a world where all would be right among God's people,
where inequalities would be corrected,
where 'too much' and 'too little' would be no more,
where God's own power would contain our human frailty.

Jesus mourns the lack of justice in the land
There was a rich man who was dressed in purple and fine linen
and who feasted sumptuously every day.
And at his gate lay a poor man named Lazarus, covered with sores,
who longed to satisfy his hunger with what fell from the rich man's table;
even the dogs would come and lick his sores. The poor man died
and was carried away by the angels to be with Abraham.
The rich man also died and was buried.
In Hades, where he was being tormented,
he looked up and saw Abraham far away with Lazarus by his side.
(Luke 16:19-23)

We pray
Praised be Jesus, revelation of God's compassion,
who shows us that God is not a distant God,
looking on, unconcerned with the world he made.
Praised be Jesus, who feels and acts on the pain of the poor
and the sorrow of those who suffer
and the indignity of the innocent victim.

We are called to dream God's dream
It is a fact that men and women in various parts of the world
feel personally affected by the injustices and violations of human rights
committed in distant countries, places they may never visit.
When interdependence is recognised in this way,
the correlative response is solidarity.
Solidarity is not a feeling of vague compassion or shallow distress
at the misfortunes of so many people both near and far.
It is a firm and persevering determination to commit oneself
to the common good, to the good of all and of each individual,
because we are all really responsible for all.
(John Paul II)

We pray
Praised be God's Spirit, the Spirit of Resurrection,
awakening God's dream in our hearts,
inspiring in us a sense of solidarity,
freeing our hearts to rise above our own ego,
freeing our hearts to feel for others,
freeing our hearts to pursue God's justice in the world.

Glory be …

Planning in the Parish

Reading through these passages, consider which of them speaks to you about planning in the parish:

With all wisdom and insight, he has made known to us
the mystery of his will, according to his good pleasure
which he set forth in Christ, as a plan for the fulness of time,
to gather up all things in him, things in heaven and things on earth.
(Ephesians 1:8-10)

Then the kingdom of heaven will be like this.
Ten bridesmaids took their lamps and went to meet the bridegroom.
Five of them were foolish and five were wise.
When the foolish took their lamps, they took no oil with them;
but the wise took flasks of oil with their lamps.
(Matthew 25:1-4)

The wind blows where it chooses, and you hear the sound of it,
but you do now know where it comes from or where it goes.
So it is with everyone who is born of the Spirit.
(John 3:8)

No one sews a piece of unshrunk cloth on an old cloak,
for the patch pulls away from the cloak and a worse tear is made.
Neither is new wine put into old wineskins; otherwise,
the skins burst and the wine is spilled and the skins are destroyed;
but new wine is put into fresh wineskins, and so both are preserved.
(Matthew 9:16-17)

Thomas said to him, 'Lord, we do not know where you are going;
how can we know the way?' Jesus said to him,
'I am the way, and the truth, and the life.
(John 14:4-6)

Let anyone who has an ear
listen to what the Spirit is saying to the churches.
(Revelation 2:11)

A woman named Martha welcomed him into her home.
She had a sister named Mary, who sat at the Lord's feet
and listened to what he was saying.
But Martha was distracted by her many tasks.
(Luke 10:38-40)

'For which of you, intending to build a tower, does not first sit down
and estimate the cost, to see whether he has enough to complete it?
Otherwise, when he has laid a foundation and is not able to finish,
all who see it will begin to ridicule him, saying,
'This fellow began to build and was not able to finish.'
(Luke 14:28-30)

Prayer
Lord, as we work together planning for the future well-being of our parish,
we pray that all our work may be focused on you.

At the heart of what we do, may there be listening,
listening to what your Spirit in saying to us,
through our people and through the world around us.

At the heart of what we are dong, may there be wisdom,
wisdom that does everything with care and forethought,
wisdom that is shrewd and astute.

At the heart of what we are doing, may there be courage,
courage to explore and to experiment,
courage to let go and courage to begin again.

Lord, lead us along your path.
May we work as if everything depended on us
and await the outcome as if everything depended on you.

Glory be …

How does Easter Begin? (1)

Scripture
Now when they heard this
(the proclamation that Jesus was risen),
they were cut to the heart
and said to Peter and to the other apostles,
'Brothers, what should we do?'
Peter said to them, 'Repent and be baptised every one of you
in the name of Jesus Christ,
so that your sins may be forgiven;
and you will receive the gift of the Holy Spirit.'
(Acts 2:37-38)

Reflection
Easter week can be such an anti-climax.
Ash Wednesday had a sense of new beginnings.
Lent was a project, a spiritual challenge.
We strove, we faltered, perhaps we picked up again.
Holy Week was a crescendo, Easter a culmination.
Then nothing. Back to normal. 'Ordinary time.'

In fact, Easter week should be everything –
as it was with the first disciples.
And it should be for us what it was for them –
a beginning and not a conclusion;
an awakening and not a tapering off.

When Peter proclaimed to the people
the good news that Jesus was risen,
those with whom he struck a chord – who were 'cut to the heart' –
asked, 'What shall we do?' His answer – 'Repent.'

He was speaking from experience.
By the lakeside he had encountered the risen Lord.
Three times he had professed, 'I love you' –
wiping out the threefold betrayal
that had left their relationship ending in failure.
Easter for Peter was reconciliation –
and the beginning of repentance.

Prayer
Response: Come Lord Jesus!

May our Easter joy let loose and set in train
a process of conversion in our lives.
Just at the penance of Lent was a preparation for Easter,
may our repentance now be our response to Easter,
the new life of Easter coming to birth in our souls.

Like Peter, we arrive at Easter in our failure and fragility.
Help us, Lord, to see Easter as New Beginning,
with a liberating feeling of being forgiven.

May we begin each day as if it were Easter day,
bathed in a spirit of forgiveness and reconciliation,
bringing that spirit and peace to the world.

Easter for Peter was reconciliation and peace
with a dear friend who had died.
As our dear departed experience God's kingdom,
may we experience ourselves at peace with them.

Glory be …

How does Easter Begin? (2)

Scripture
So they went out
(Mary Magdalene, and Mary the mother of James, and Salome)
and fled from the tomb,
for terror and amazement had seized them;
and they said nothing to anyone,
for they were afraid.
(Mark 16:8)

Reflection
When the first disciples to reach the tomb discovered it was empty
and were addressed by the angel, they were filled,
not with joy or relief or exhilaration,
but with terror and amazement and fear.

Easter had happened, had begun.
But they were only beginning to sense it.
It was only beginning to break through.
Coming to the tomb,
there was a cloud of gloom and disappointment.
Coming from the tomb,
there was confusion and bewilderment.
Too soon for joy.

Easter begins slowly.
More like a dawn than a flash of lightning.
Its light penetrates only gradually
through the darkness, the mist, the clouds.

Quiet

Prayer

Lord, Easter begins now
and 'now' means me as I am
and not as I might ideally be.
Easter dawns on me as I am;
it dawns on my fear as well as my confidence,
on my failed as well as my successful self,
on my confusion as well as my clarity.

May Easter come gradually to birth in me;
may its light reach into my darkness;
may its life reach into my death.

May I allow Easter to dawn in me;
may I be expectant, passionate for its coming;
may I be patient, acknowledging its pace;
may I be confident, sure of its power.

For our church, which confidently proclaims
the good news of Easter,
that Easter's dawn may penetrate its clouds and mist
and break through wherever it experiences
gloom and disappointment.

For all who are confused or disappointed
through the circumstances and experiences of their lives,
that others around them, with a sense of Easter,
may rekindle their trust in the light.

Glory be ...

Preparing for a Parish Assembly

Scripture
This is one of the earliest 'assemblies' of Christians we know of. The issue was momentous – the inclusion of Gentiles in God's plan. There were differences, but also listening. There emerged a sense of what the Spirit was saying, and a decision about which there was peace.

When Paul and Barnabas came to Jerusalem,
they were welcomed by the church and the apostles and the elders …
But some believers who belonged to the sect of the Pharisees
stood up and said, 'It is necessary for them to be circumcised
and ordered to keep the law of Moses'.

The apostles and elders met together to consider this matter.
After there had been much debate Peter stood up and said to them,
'You know that in the early days God made a choice among you,
that I should be the one through whom the Gentiles would hear
the message of the good news and become believers.
And God, who knows the human heart, testified to them
by giving them the Holy Spirit, just as he did to us;
and in cleansing their hearts by faith
he has made no distinction between them and us.
Now therefore why are you putting God to the test
by placing on the neck of the disciples a yoke
that neither our ancestors nor we have been able to bear?
On the contrary, we believe that we will be saved through the grace
of the Lord Jesus, just as they will.'

The whole assembly kept silence, and listened to Barnabas and Paul
as they told of all the signs and wonders
that God had done through them among the Gentiles.
After they finished speaking, James replied,
'Simeon has related how God first looked favourably on the Gentiles,
to take from among them a people for his name.
This agrees with the words of the prophets … Therefore

I have reached the decision that we should not trouble those Gentiles
who are turning to God, but we should write to them
to abstain only from things polluted by idols and from fornication
and from whatever has been strangled and from blood.'
(Acts 15:4-20)

Prayers
We pray that the Spirit of this momentous Christian gathering
will inspire us too, as we gather in the Lord.

Response: Lord, pour out your Spirit upon us.

We give you thanks, O Lord, for your Spirit
guiding our preparations and inspiring our wisdom.

We pray that there will be good listening at our gathering
and that the collective wisdom of God's people will show itself.

We pray for creativity of thought
and a sense of new life at our gathering.

We pray for God's Spirit to inspire us as we talk and listen
and to guide us in the right direction.

We pray for a spirit of energy and enthusiasm
that will last long after in our parish.

Together
Spirit in our midst, awaken us into new vitality;
arouse us with new energy; enthuse us with new conviction;
link us in a spirit of togetherness; guide us in a spirit of wisdom;
support us in a spirit of encouragement;
inspire us, we pray, as co-workers
in the coming about of God's Kingdom
unveiled among us by Jesus the Lord.

Glory be ...

Visiting in the Parish

Every doorstep is holy ground
Moses was keeping the flock of his father-in-law Jethro,
the priest of Midian; he led his flock beyond the wilderness
and came to Horeb, the mountain of God.
There the angel of the Lord appeared to him
in a flame of fire out of a bush;
he looked and the bush was blazing, yet it was not consumed.
Then Moses said, 'I must turn aside and look at this great sight
and see why the bush is not burned up.'
When the Lord saw that he had turned aside to see,
God called to him out of the bush, 'Moses, Moses!'
And he said, 'Here I am.' Then he said, 'Come no closer!
Remove the sandals from your feet,
for the place on which you are standing is holy ground.'
(Exodus 3:1-5)

Prayer
Moses removed his sandals,
to acknowledge that he was standing on holy ground.
Each home in our parish is also holy ground.
As we stand on the doorstep, may we bring with us
a deep respect for God's people who live there.

Visiting – a special moment in the bible
In those days Mary set out and went with haste
to a Judean town in the hill country, where she entered
the house of Zechariah and greeted Elizabeth.
When Elizabeth heard Mary's greeting, the child leaped in her womb.
And Elizabeth was filled with the Holy Spirit
and exclaimed with a loud cry, 'Blessed are you among women
and blessed is the fruit of your womb.
And why has this happened to me,

that the mother of my Lord comes to me?
For as soon as I heard the sound of your greeting,
the child in my womb leaped for joy.'
(Luke 1:39-44)

Prayer
Mary's visiting Elizabeth was a time of surprise and joy and happiness,
a time when God was near. May it be so when we visit.
May people sense the nearness of God.
May we increase the happiness in people's lives.

Paul and Apollos visited the people of Corinth, bringing good news
What then is Apollos? What is Paul?
Servants through whom you came to believe,
as the Lord assigned to each.
I planted, Apollos watered, but God gave the growth.
So neither the one who plants nor the one who waters is anything,
but only God who gives the growth ...
For we are God's servants, working together;
you are God's field, God's building.
(1 Corinthians 3:5-7, 9)

Prayer
When we visit in the parish, may we rely on God
who will be with us at each moment.
We pledge ourselves to giving it our best –
and we await with confidence the growth that God will give.

Recalling the gospel mystery of visitation, we pray together;
Our Father ...
Hail Mary ...
Glory be ...

Care and Compassion

Scripture
'Come to me, all you that are weary
and are carrying heavy burdens
and I will give you rest.
Take my yoke upon you and learn from me
for I am gentle and humble in heart
and you will find rest for your souls.
For my yoke is easy and my burden is light.'
(Matthew 11:28-30)

Reflection
Jesus' *words* are filled with compassion.
Jesus' *actions* are filled with compassion.

In his *words* – his stories, his teachings –
he imagines a world built on compassion.

In the story of the prodigal son
the father was 'filled with compassion'.
In the story of the good Samaritan
that man was 'moved with pity' and inspired to care.

In Jesus' *actions*, his words become real and active
and his dream begins to take flesh.

When he sees the crowds, he 'feels pity' for them
and sets out to teach them.
When he encounters the widow at Nain,
he 'had compassion for her' and acted.

In his care and compassion
Jesus is filled with the feelings of God for God's people.
In Jesus, God's compassion in poured out in the world.
In Jesus, God's compassion takes flesh.

Prayers
Response: May all God's people feel God's care.

For all in our parish, in our common need
of the ministry of care and compassion.
We reach out to touch with our prayer
those whose need touches our hearts.

We pray for ourselves, as we listen to Jesus saying to us,
'Come to me, all you that are weary and carry heavy burdens.'

For our world in its need for care and compassion.
May there be an end to numbness and uncaring.
May God's compassion, working through our hearts,
dispel the world's numbness to need.

All
Fill us, O God, with the Spirit that filled Jesus,
your Spirit of care and compassion,
to be our rest when we are over-burdened,
and to be our gift to others in their trouble.

Glory be ...

God Words

This prayer, inspired by Walter Brueggemann, is about the words – verbs, adjectives, nouns – that Israel drew on to speak about God.

Our God – a God who CREATES
By the word of the Lord the heavens were made
and all their host by the breath of his mouth.
(Psalm 33:6)

O creator God, we reflect on your creativity in our midst;
we call you POTTER – and allow ourselves to be shaped by you;
we call you VINEDRESSER – and await your designs for us;
we call you MOTHER – and rest in your embrace.

Our God – a God who PROMISES
Reside in this land as an alien and I will be with you and bless you
for to you and to your descendants I will give all these lands
and I will fulfil the oath that I swore to your father Abraham.
(Genesis 26:3)

O God of future and promise, we reflect on your unfailing loyalty;
we call you FAITHFUL – be our rock and our fortress;
we call you STEADFAST LOVE – be our ultimate assurance;
we call you TRUE – be our model for imitation.

Our God – a God who DELIVERS
I am the Lord and I will free you from the burdens of the Egyptians
and deliver you from slavery to them. I will redeem you
with an outstretched arm and with mighty acts of judgement.
(Exodus 6:6)

You who deliver your people, we reflect on your saving power amongst us;
we call you MERCIFUL and SLOW TO ANGER – forgive our sins;
we call you HEALER – soothe our pain;
we call you REDEEMER, LIBERATOR – show us the path to freedom.

Our God – a God who COMMANDS
Now therefore, if you obey my voice and keep my covenant
you shall be my treasured possession out of all the peoples.
(Exodus 19:5)

O God who commands our obedience, we reflect on your rule in our lives;
we call you JUDGE – may we listen attentively to your word;
we call you KING – may we reflect your justice in our relationships
we call you FATHER – may we practise your compassion.

Our God – a God who LEADS
He leads me beside still waters, he restores my soul.
He leads me in right paths for his name's sake.
(Psalm 23:2-3)

You who show us the path of life, we reflect on your providence;
we call you SHEPHERD – help those who are without help;
you FEED us – feed those who have no food;
you COMFORT us – bring solace in all distress;
you GUIDE us – guide those who are without a way.

Prayer
Our words, O Lord, cannot exhaust your wonder.
Only your Word fully expresses who you are.
We bless you in Christ,
the new creation,
the fulfilment of your promise,
our redeemer,
who gives us the new commandment
and leads us in the way of your kingdom,
you who live and reign over all ages. Amen.

Letting Go

JESUS LETS GO

Scripture
'You will receive power when the Holy Spirit has come upon you;
and you will be my witnesses in Jerusalem, in all Judea and Samaria
and to the ends of the earth.'
When he had said this, as they were watching,
he was lifted up and a cloud took him out of their sight.
(Acts 1:8-9)

'I will give you the keys of the kingdom of heaven
and whatever you bind on earth will be bound in heaven
and whatever you loose on earth will be loosed in heaven.'
(Matthew 16:19)

Reflection
God's way since creating the world
has been to invite our co-operation, our co-creating
as partners in divine creativity.
Maybe Jesus could have left detailed instructions
about how to run a church.
But his way was God's way
and so instead he left his Spirit.
Trusting us, he let go and left it to us
to continue treading his path,
to continue the work of the kingdom
as faithful disciples.

WE LET GO

Scripture
Peter answered him, 'Lord, if it is you,
command me to come to you on the water.'
He said, 'Come'. So Peter got out of the boat,
started walking on the water and came towards Jesus.
But when he noticed the strong wind he became frightened
and beginning to sink, he cried out, 'Lord save me!'
Jesus immediately reached out his hand and caught him,
saying to him, 'You of little faith, why did you doubt?'
(Matthew 14:28-31)

Reflection
We see Jesus' trust in us
entrusting to us the work of God's kingdom.
But we can only embrace this trust
by entrusting ourselves to him.
We can only respond to his letting go
by letting go ourselves,
by trusting in his power
and not relying on ourselves alone.

We pray, in our little faith
to let go into his arms,
to let go, into his plan,
to let go, into his power,
to let go, into his future.

Glory be …

Paradoxes

These are some of the paradoxes that are experienced in parish life and in the work of pastoral renewal. The temptation is to collapse the paradox by choosing one side over the other. The challenge is to live the paradox and enjoy the journey!

ACTION AND REFLECTION

Most groups have their 'doers' and their 'thinkers'.
Some want to tease things out, to talk and to imagine.
Others want to get down to action.
But we need both.
Without the doers, we become a talk shop;
without the thinkers, we become mindless activists.

Lord, give us a deep appreciation of each other's giftedness,
of those with the gift of practicality, like Martha,
and those with the gift of reflection, like Mary.
May we experience the enrichment that this diversity brings.

OPTIMISM AND PESSIMISM

Sometimes we can feel very optimistic;
we see such signs of hope around us
in the church and in the world.
Other times, we can feel quite pessimistic;
with so much inertia and complacency,
we wonder how we are going to survive.

Lord, bless us with the virtue of hope,
somewhere between presumption and despair.
Bless us with confidence in your providence at work,
and also with a sober realism
about the challenges that face us.

OUR WORK AND GOD'S WORK
Thomas said to Jesus, 'Lord, we do not know
where you are going; how can we know the way?'
Do we sometimes change one little word and say,
'We do not know where *we* are going'?
So that it becomes our way and not the Lord's,
our work and not the work of the Spirit?

Lord, may all that we do be filled with a lively sense
of all that you do, in us and in our midst.
And in our total dependence on you may we realise
how much you depend on us.

PATIENCE AND URGENCY
Jesus said, 'I came to bring fire to the earth
and how I wish it were already kindled'
– his urgency reverberates in me.
Jesus also said, 'So do not worry about tomorrow'
– and his serenity echoes in me.

Lord, make me both patient and urgent.
May I trust in the slow, but sure onset of your reign;
may I trust in the creative slowness of true growth.
And may I also be impelled with enthusiasm,
with an eagerness that cries, 'Your kingdom come!'

Prayer
Help us, Lord, to live with paradox,
to suffer uncertainty and contradiction
with a firm confidence in you.

Glory be …

Baptism Community

Reflection
Imagine a small group of people,
passionately dedicated to living out their vision,
their shared beliefs and values.
Imagine that somebody from outside saw how they lived
and was attracted to find out more.
Imagine this person eventually deciding to ask
if they could join the group.

Imagine the response –
the delight, the honour –
the desire to celebrate this event.
Imagine the celebration,
what it means for the newcomer
and what it means to those already in the group,
as a confirmation of their faith
and as a new spur to their living.

That is what every baptism is meant to be
in the Christian community.
That is how central baptism is.
Each newcomer is a celebration of what we all are,
revitalising our sense of who we are,
impressing on us once more the distinction of our calling.

I wonder about the reality though,
when baptism is little more than a private event,
taking place when there is nobody else around in the church.
Imagine if it were part of Sunday Eucharist;
imagine if we were delighted;
imagine if we were inspired.

Scripture
Blessed be the God and Father of our Lord Jesus Christ!
By his great mercy he has given us a new birth into a living hope
through the resurrection of Jesus Christ from the dead,
and into an inheritance that is imperishable,
undefiled and unfading, kept in heaven for you.
Although you have not seen him, you love him;
and even though you do not see him now,
you believe in him and rejoice
with an indescribable and glorious joy.
(1 Peter 1:3-4, 8)

Prayers
We pray for all those who minister in our parishes
to increase our sense of our own baptism.

We pray for baptism teams
who help prepare families for baptism
and who create a sense of welcome and belonging.

We pray for those who help prepare families
for first communion and confirmation,
so that these are real experiences of initiation
into the life of the Christian community,
into the fullness of baptised existence.

We pray for those who promote
the rite for the Christian initiation of adults,
who prepare adults and others
for entry into the community of faith.

We pray for all who minister to bring baptism alive.
We pray that that baptism will come to the centre
of our consciousness as a Christian community
and that it will be an ongoing source of renewal.

Glory be...

References

Page   Reference

20-21   Adapted from a version (by this author) that appeared in Accord, *Celebrating Marriage 2000: A Jubilee Resource Book.*

24-25   Thomas Merton, *Conjectures of a Guilty Bystander,* New York: Doubleday/Image, 1968, pages 131, 158.

28   Pope John Paul II, *The Vocation and Mission of the Lay Faithful (Christifideles Laici),* 1988, paragraph 11.

47   Isak Dinesen, 'Babette's Feast.' *Anecdotes of Destiny,* London: Penguin, 1986, page 60.

52-53   St. Augustine, Sermon 272.

65   Pope John Paul II, *The Vocation and Mission of the Lay Faithful (Christifideles Laici),* 1988, paragraph 2.

66-67   Adapted from a version (by this author) that appeared in Accord, *Celebrating Marriage 2000: A Jubilee Resource Book.*

68-69   Donagh O'Shea, *Meditations with Meister Eckhart* (cassette tape), Cork: Ennismore Publications, 1988 – adapted by the author.

72   Bishop Donal Murray, *Put Out into the Deep Water,* Lenten Pastoral, 2001.

74   R.S. Thomas, 'The Kingdom.' *Collected Poems 1945-1990,* London: Phoenix Giant, 1995, page 233.

78   Pope John Paul II, *At the Dawn of the New Millennium (Novo Millennio Ineunte),* 2001, paragraphs 15, 29.

80   Origen, *Dialogue with Heraclides,* 150.

80-81   Richard Holloway, *The Observer,* 15th April 2001.

84   Pope John Paul II, *The Vocation and Mission of the Lay Faithful (Christifideles Laici),* 1988, paragraphs 26-27.

90   Vatican Council II, *The Church in the Modern World (Gaudium et Spes),* 1965, paragraphs 22, 41.

92-93   Pope Paul VI, *Evangelisation in the Modern World (Evangelii Nuntiandi)*, 1975, paragraph 21.

94   Thomas Waldron, 'Hope and the Hungers of the Heart.' *The Furrow*, October 1992, page 525.

106   Enda Lyons, *Partnership in Parish*, Dublin: Columba Press, 1993, pages 25-26.

114-115 Anne Daly (previously unpublished).

124-125 Adapted from a version (by this author) that appeared in Accord, *Celebrating Marriage 2000: A Jubilee Resource Book.*

126-127 do.

130-131 do.

137   St Symeon of Thessalonika, *De Ordine Sepulturae*, 336.

139   Pope John Paul, *The Church's Social Concern (Solicitudo Rei Socialis)*, 1987, paragraph 38.

152   See Walter Brueggemann, *Theology of the Old Testament*, Minneapolis: Fortress Press, 1997.

Scripture quotations are from the *New Revised Standard Version.*

Index of Themes and Names

Adult faith, 32
Advent, 44
Andrew, 38
Annunciation, 46
Assembly, 146
Augustine, 52
Baptism, 28, 48, 158
Beginning, 72, 102
Body of Christ, 40, 52, 98
Bones, 34
Breath, 34
Brueggemann, Walter, 152
Building, 30
Call, calling, 50, 100, 124
Camus, Albert, 80
Care, 50, 56, 150
Catechism, 108
Church, 16, 126
Collaboration, 64, 132, 154
Commitment, 20, 100, 124
Compassion, 150
Confirmation, 106
Creed, 20
Daly, Anne, 114
Dead, 136
Dinesen, Isak, 47
Discernment, 26
Dream, 12
Easter, 80, 122, 124
Eckhart, Meister, 46, 68
Enough, 14
Eucharist, 22, 134
Evangelisation, 70, 92, 128

Faith, 32
Fruits of Spirit, 58
Gifts, 40, 98
God, 24, 94, 152
Holloway, Richard, 80
Hospitality, 42, 76, 148
Initiation, Christian, 28, 48, 52, 106, 158
John Paul II, 28, 65, 78, 84, 139
John, 122
Justice, 138
Kingdom, 74
Letting go, 154
Listening, 62, 94
Love, 20, 100
Luke, 120
Lyons, Enda, 106
Mark, 118
Mary, 46
Matthew, 116
Meditation, 60, 96
Merton, Thomas, 24
Ministry, 18, 56, 86, 98
Mission, 70, 92, 128
Morning, 88
Murray, Donal, 72
Names, 108
O'Shea, Donagh, 68
Offertory, 134
Older people, 130
Opened, 48
Origen, 80
Outreach, 68, 76, 148
Parables, 16

Paradoxes, 156
Parish, 12, 30, 84, 114, 146, 158
Partnership, 64, 132, 154
Paths, 36
Paul VI, 92
Planning, 78, 170
'Point vierge', 24
Rain, 104
Reaching out/in, 68
Reconciliation, 126
Resurrection, 80, 142, 144
Saints, 136
Searching, 16
Seen and unseen, 54
Separated people, 66
Service, 86
Setting out, 72, 102
Shepherd, 50
Souls, 136
Spirit, 10, 34, 58

Spring, 104
Still, 82
Symeon, 137
Teresa of Avila, 52
Thanks, 18
Thomas, R.S., 74
Trinity, 112
Trust, 154
Vatican II, 90
Vision, 12
Visiting, 76, 148
Vocation, 50, 100, 124
You are, 90
Waldron, Thomas, 94
Welcome, 42, 110, 76, 148
Widowed people, 66
Wisdom, 26
Witness, 92
Words, 152

Index of Scripture Passages

Genesis
26:3, 152

Exodus
3:1-5, 148
3:7-8, 62
6:6, 152
16:15-18, 138
18:13-14, 18, 21-22, 64
19:5, 153
22:23, 95

Numbers
11:11-14, 16-17, 64

Deuteronomy
1:32-33, 37
30:15-16, 19-20, 124

Job
24:12, 95

Psalms
5:3, 88
16:11, 37
23:2-3, 153
32:8, 37
33:6, 152
46:1-3, 6, 10, 82
59:16, 88
84:5, 37
104:30, 102
116:1-2, 95
143:8, 88

Isaiah
9:2, 44
40:3, 37, 44
43:1, 109
43:18-19, 102
44:2-5, 104
46:3-4, 130
49:15-16, 109
51:10, 37
56:5, 109
62:2-3, 109

Jeremiah
6:16, 37

Ezekiel
34:11-17, 50
34:26-27, 105
37:1-14, 34

Hosea
6:2-3, 104

Habbakuk
1:2, 95

Wisdom
6:12-13, 26

Matthew
2:8, 110
2:13-15, 116
5:14-16, 54

6:3-4, 6, 17-18, 54
9:16-17, 140
10:40, 111
11:28-30, 110, 150
13:44-45, 117
14:15-20, 14
14:28-31, 155
16:19, 154
18:19-20, 117
21:28-31, 116
25:1-4, 140

Mark
1:14-15, 74
1:35, 88
2:13-17, 42
4:26-29, 118
4:35-41, 82
7:32-35, 119
7:32-37, 48
8:22-25, 118
10:14, 111
10:14-15, 32
10:42-45, 86
14:3, 56
16:2, 4-6, 88
16:8, 144

Luke
1:38, 110
1:39-44, 148
6:34-35, 120
7:36-38, 56
10:1-2, 65
10:1-12, 76
10:20, 108
10:38, 110
10:38-40, 141
12:6-7, 96
12:49, 12
14:12-14, 120
14:27-30, 120

14:28-30, 141
15:2, 110
15:20, 111
16:19-21, 111
16:19-23, 138
17:7-10, 86
17:11-19, 18
18:1-7, 121
21:1-4, 134

John
1:1-5, 14, 122
1:11-12, 110
1:35-42, 38
3:8, 11, 140
5:2-6, 123
6:8-9, 134
10:10, 12
10:11, 14-15, 50
11:38-39, 43-44, 80, 123
12:1-3, 56
12:20-25, 39
14:4-6, 140
14:5, 37
15:5, 114
20:20-22, 106
20:26-29, 122

Acts of the Apostles
1:8-9, 154
2:37-38, 142
6:1-6, 26
11:1-18, 70
15:4-20, 147

Romans
8:26-27, 10
10:14-15, 128
12:1, 134
12:4-8, 40
13:11-12, 88
15:7, 111

1 Corinthians
2:10-12, 10
3:5-7, 9, 149
3:9-11, 16-17, 30
7:17, 100
9:16, 92
12:4-7, 113
12:8-11, 40
12:14-20, 98
13:11-12, 32

2 Corinthians
5:16-20, 28
5:17-18, 127

Galatians
5:22, 58

Ephesians
1:8-10, 140
2:19-22, 136
4:11-12, 40
4:14-15, 32

Philippians
2:2-7, 86

Hebrews
11:8, 72

James
5:7-8, 105

1 Peter
1:3-4, 8, 159
2:4-5, 30

1 John
3:14, 20

Revelation
2:11, 140
21:5, 102